KU-065-894

Penguin Education

Cultural Action for Freedom

Paulo Freire

Paulo Freire, until recently a Fellow of the Center for the
Study of Development and Social Change and a Visiting
Professor at Harvard's Center for Studies in Education and
Development, is now serving as Special Consultant to the
Office of Education of the World Council of Churches in
Geneva. In Chile, he served as consultant to UNESCO's
Institute of Research and Training in Agrarian Reform
(ICIRA), and also as Professor at the University of Chile.
Prior to that, in Brazil, he was Secretary of Education and
General Coordinator of the National Plan of Adult Literacy.
His first book, *Educação como Prática da Liberdade*
was published in Brazil in 1967 and his most recent,
Pedagogy of the Oppressed (also available in Penguin),
appeared in English translation in 1970.

Cultural Action for Freedom

Paulo Freire

Penguin Education

Penguin Education
A Division of Penguin Books Ltd,
Harmondsworth, Middlesex, England
Penguin Books Inc, 7110 Ambassador Road
Baltimore, Md 21207, USA
Penguin Books Australia Ltd,
Ringwood, Victoria, Australia

First published as a monograph in the USA by the
Harvard Educational Review, 1970
Published by Penguin Books 1972
Reprinted 1974
Copyright © Center for the Study of Development and
Social Change, Cambridge, Massachussets, 1970

Made and printed in Great Britain by
C. Nicholls & Company Ltd
Set in Monotype Times

Contents

Preface

Here is a voice from that Third World which is so often spoken of but itself seldom speaks. What is more, this voice speaks neither to the Third World alone nor to the powers that be in the 'mother countries'. It is not a voice of representation, petition or remonstrance. Its message, which began to spread in Latin America some years ago, is today being heard and finds an echo among those sectors of the First World which, for one reason or another, feel attuned to the Third.

Something has happened since Frantz Fanon wrote *The Wretched of the Earth*. When that book appeared, in the early sixties, Jean-Paul Sartre noted with some alarm: he is not talking to us. In Fanon, said Sartre, the Third World had found itself and was speaking *to* itself; it was not concerned with the master world. Nevertheless, Sartre went on, the master world, the Europeans, would do well to take heed of what the man was saying, if they cared for their own survival.

In the voice of Paulo Freire the Third World still disdains to address itself to the managers of the First. In his opinion, and in that of many of his peers, there can be no dialogue between antagonists. But Freire invites the hitherto silent sectors of the affluent world or at least the more awakened members of those over-managed, over-consuming societies to a rediscovery of the world in which they live and of their own vocation in that world, in dialogue with its pariahs. That his invitation did not fall on deaf ears was demonstrated by the enthusiastic response of students and other minorities to his brief visit to the United States in 1969. The Centre for the Study of Development and Social Change which with the cooperation of many others made

that visit possible was convinced that an encounter of Paulo
Freire with the American reality, and of the actors in the struggling grass-roots movements with his thought and personality,
could only have salutary effects. It was not mistaken.

The thought of Paulo Freire is essentially a situated thought
and any attempt to promote it to an abstract universality, on the
grounds of the acknowledged efficiency of his literacy method, at
once misrepresents and disfigures it. The situation which
engendered the Freire approach – as he himself takes pains to
explain in his introduction – is the emergence of the popular
masses into the national political scene in the so-called 'underdeveloped' countries, more precisely in Latin America. In the
global context, the situation is that of the emergence of the Third
World onto the stage of contemporary history. This is a situation pregnant with the most exciting as well as the most dismal
possibilities. The decolonization of the Third World opens the
way either to the true liberation of all mankind or to its more
efficient domestication. It is a situation, therefore, which calls
for a reappraisal of the meaning and methods of education.

In a way, this can be said to be what the debate around
'development' is all about. Clearly this is more than just another ideological debate. It is far more than a struggle between
opposing economic or political interests. At issue are divergent
images of man, or more correctly, an already established image
which its keepers are attempting to prescribe for others and a
new image which is struggling to be. In this way the thought of
Paulo Freire finds its link with what has been described as 'the
making of a counter-culture' and with the search for a definition
and method of radical education. The debate carries us to the
very sources of our humanity. That is why Freire introduces his
method of alphabetization with a digression into the philosophical presuppositions of his pedagogy.

The cardinal principle of that philosophy is man's vocation to
be more – more, that is, than what he is at any given time or
place. There are thus no developed men except in a biological

sense. The essence of the human is to be in a continual non-natural process. In other words, the characteristic of the human species is its repeatedly demonstrated capacity for transcending what is merely given, what is purely determined.

Man's vocation realizes itself in his praxis, which transforms and expresses the world. In its turn, this praxis, which is action and language, turns back upon man and 'overdetermines' him; that is to say, it conditions him and defines the horizon of meanings within which his further action is to take place. Education – like all other processes of socialization – tends to reinforce this 'overdetermination'. From the inherent ambivalence of education, namely, its capacity to bring out what is least determined in man as well as to programme and determine him, Paulo Freire derives what I think is his fundamental thesis: that there is no neutral education. Education is either for domestication or for freedom. Although it is customarily conceived as a conditioning process, education can equally be an instrument for de-conditioning. An initial choice is required of the educator.

Education can be de-conditioning because man, essentially a conditioned being, is also essentially a being capable of knowing what conditions him, capable of reflecting on his action and behaviour, and of perceiving his perceptions. The key to 'perception of perception', and hence to the recuperation of hidden or mystified reality, is problematization. Problematization, which means both asking questions and calling into question and is therefore a challenging attitude, is, at one and the same time, the beginning of an authentic act of knowing and the beginning of an act of subversion of 'overdetermination', that is, subversion of praxis inverted upon man.

Problematization does not come easily to silent, passively receptive masses, no matter where they are – in the 'countryside' of the world or in the classrooms or before the television sets of the 'cities'. A key role is therefore to be played by the revolutionary educator, whose task is to challenge both the students and the reality which is to be studied. The 'theory' or 'theoretical context' of problematization is dialogue, that is, the examination and appropriation of mediating reality by conscious actors who stand in a subject-to-subject relationship to one another.

This theoretical context may, however, degenerate into ideology, which is the opposite of dialogue. Ideology is doctrine or theory which is administratively preserved and transmitted. There is therefore a permanent need of dialogue for dismantling bureaucratic constructions and for preventing the entrenchment of vested interests.

It is not surprising that the Freire method has reportedly produced spectacular results among illiterate peasants in Latin America and has touched responsive chords among marginal or disaffected groups in the industrial world. Nor is it difficult to see why a method based on such a philosophy would be received with caution, if not alarm, by the holders of political or academic power. The truth is that at the heart of the thought of Paulo Freire there is an experience and a vivid perception of what he calls the 'culture of silence' and at the core of his project the decision to subvert it. This 'culture of silence' – which is yet to be accurately described and structurally analysed – has for its distinguishing mark its prescriptive character: it is dictation, communiqué, 'information' – in short, pre-processed and pre-digested reality.

The Third World has long subsisted on such pre-empted definitions not only of reality as such, but of its own historical reality. Such pre-masticated food is usually the fare of dependent, 'object' beings, beings who are not, or not yet beings for themselves, but for another. The Third World has not only had its history made for it but the meaning thereof defined by another. In fact, the Third World could adequately be described as the 'object' world *par excellence*: it is the world which was 'discovered', invaded, subjugated, governed, then educated, converted and 'assisted' by another. The purpose of this systematic concern and action was its pacification. The pacification of the Third World under the beneficent rule of the First has been and remains the theme of recent history. Not only armies and civil services but churches and universities have contributed to this unprecedented undertaking.

The challenge of Paulo Freire – and his is one of a growing number of voices – is for the oppressed of the First as well as the Third World to rediscover that history and its essentially inhuman character, and to join hands in the construction of a truly human and universal history.

It seems unnecessary to emphasise the utopian nature of this call and this pedagogy, utopian not in the sense that they are unrealizable but in that they unite in a single perspective the denunciation of a dehumanizing reality and the annunciation of a possibly more human one, and are thus primarily turned towards the future. But utopian also – it must be added – in the sense that the forces of the established order arrayed against them are all too powerful and cannot lightly be discounted. The nations now irrupting into history carry, not only in their economies and political systems but in the mentalities of their present rulers, the marks of centuries of efforts toward their pacification. The mass media and schools of the director societies produce an unrelenting flow of communication and prescription which few of them show any signs of being able to resist. The North and West persist in claiming the right to define the truth of the East and South, and what is called 'under-development' is at its deepest root a state of prostration of the spirit: objectively, a situation so defined by an overbearing culture and, subjectively, the condition of a mind which has meekly internalized its prescriptions.

There begin, however, to appear signs that the 'object' world is stirring and there is a spreading feeling that the truth of the First World may not be found in its own self-authenticated definitions but in the lives and consciousness of its victims. The examples of China, Cuba and Tanzania have not been lost, nor have the unbelievable suffering and courage of the Vietnamese passed unnoticed. There are people who are speaking of a new language to redefine the reality which we live. It is to them, wherever they are, that the voice of Paulo Freire is addressed.

João da Veiga Coutinho

Introduction

I think it is important – for my own sake as well as the reader's – to try, at the very outset, to clarify some points fundamental to the general understanding of my ideas on education as cultural action for freedom.

This is all the more important since one of the basic aims of this work, where the process of adult literacy is discussed, is to show that if our option is *for man*, education is cultural action for freedom and therefore an act of knowing and not of memorization. This act can never be accounted for in its complex totality by a mechanistic theory, for such a theory does not perceive education in general and adult literacy in particular as an act of knowing. Instead, it reduces the practice of education to a complex of techniques, naïvely considered to be neutral, by means of which the educational process is standardized in a sterile and bureaucratic operation.

This is not a gratuitous assertion. We will later clarify the radical distinction between knowing and memorizing and the reasons why we attach such importance to the adult literacy process.

But first, some words about the socio-historical conditioning of the thinking presented here, as well as an explanation of the necessity for critical reflection on such conditioning.

From a non-dualistic viewpoint, thought and language, constituting a whole, always refer to the reality of the thinking subject. Authentic thought-language is generated in the dialectical relationship between the subject and his concrete historical and cultural reality. In the case of the alienated cultural processes characteristic of dependent or object societies, thought-language itself is alienated, whence the fact that these societies do not manifest an authentic thought of their own during the periods of most acute alienation. Reality as it is thought does not correspond to the reality being lived objectively, but rather to the reality in which the alienated man imagines himself to be. This thought is not an effective instrument either in objective reality, to which alienated man does not relate as thinking subject, or in the imagined and longed for reality. Dissociated from the action implied by authentic thought, this mode of thought is lost in ineffective, false words. Irresistibly attracted by the life style of the director society, alienated man is a nostalgic man, never truly committed to his world. To appear to be rather than to be is one of his alienated wishes. His thinking and the way he expresses the world are generally a reflection of the thought and expression of the director society.[1] His alienated culture prevents him from understanding that his thinking and world-expression cannot find acceptance beyond his frontiers unless he is faithful to his particular world. Only to the extent that he reflectively feels and knows his own particular world for having experienced it as mediation of a collective transforming praxis, only to that extent will his thought and expression gain significance beyond that world.

Such awareness of oneself and the world, however, is not the result of a purely private choice, but of an historical process in which object societies, some more rapidly than others due to

1. These managing societies in their turn usually suffer, as is natural, from the contrary illness: they are convinced of the infallibility of their thought, and for this reason find it normal that it should be piously followed by the dependent societies. In saying this we merely underline an obvious fact: in the relationship between metropolitan and dependent societies, the alienation of the latter (which implies what Guerreiro Ramos calls *exemplarism*) corresponds to the lordly manner of the former. In either case, however, one must refrain from absolutizing the statement, for just as among the alienated there are those who think in a non-alienated manner, there are unlordly denizens of the metropolises. In both cases, for different reasons, they break with the norms of their respective contexts.

the structural transformations they undergo, reflect upon
themselves and perceive themselves to be dependent. These
moments, which characterize the transitional stage of such
societies, are both problematic and creative. They testify
to the emergence of the masses and to their clamouring
presence in the historical process in varying degrees of intensity.[2]

This popular presence naturally creates a new life style in the
society. It begins to reveal society's internal and external contradictions, formerly undetected both by the masses and the
so-called intelligentsia. In this way the alienated culture begins
to be judged. Certain intellectuals begin to change their former
view of society, really discovering society's structure for the
first time. What alienation defined as the intrinsic inferiority of
the popular masses is now objectively recognized to be the
result of alienation itself, which is discovered as the manifestation of a situation of domination. Thus the more the alienated
culture is uncovered, the more the oppressive reality in which it
originates is exposed. A twofold pattern emerges. On the one

2. This process of transition also takes place in its own way in metropolitan societies, which give an appearance of unshakeable stability.
There also we see the emergence of the most depressed popular sectors,
which previously did not exist as problems, hidden as they were in their
society's affluence. As they emerge, these groups make their presence felt
by the power structures, whether by organizing themselves to give simple
witness to their inescapable presence in the historical process, or by the
most aggressive forms of political pressure.

Student groups which for a long time concentrated on purely academic
demands gradually come to share the restlessness of the oppressed
groups. The same happens to the most progressive among the intellectuals. Thus the entire scheme of metropolitan societies begins to be called
into question.

It is true that in speaking of the process of social change within these
societies, one has to take into account their greater capacity for absorbing
dissent due to their far more advanced technology. Marcuse has repeatedly called attention to the fact that this technological power is able to
transform many of these protest movements into mere manifestations of
folklore. This point, however, is not part of our subject, nor can it be
adequately dealt with in a simple footnote.

hand, the culturally alienated society as a whole is dependent on the society which oppresses it and whose economic and cultural interests it serves. At the same time, within the alienated society itself, a regime of oppression is imposed upon the masses by the power elites which in certain cases are the same as the external elites and in others are the external transformed by a kind of metastasis into domestic power groups.

In either case there is a fundamental dimension to these societies resulting from their colonial phase: their culture was established and maintained as a 'culture of silence'.[3] Here again, the twofold pattern is apparent. Externally, the alienated society as a whole, as the mere object of the director society, is not heard by the latter. On the contrary the metropolis prescribes its word, thereby effectively silencing it. Meanwhile, within the alienated society itself, the masses are subjected to the same kind of silence by the power elites.

When the popular masses get beyond the stage of fascination with their own emergence, and from demand to demand announce by their action that they are nearing a stage of sufficient organization to be able to break their submissive silence, the power elites violently attempt to arrest the process.[4] And if the elites lack the power to return the masses to their original silence, the director society, 'invited' or not, takes it upon itself to do so.

The repression used to return the masses to their silence is preceded and accompanied by a myth-making effort to identify as diabolical all thought-language which uses such words as *alienation, domination, oppression, liberation, humanization* and

3. On the 'culture of silence', see my 'Cultural Freedom in Latin America'.

4. Even a cursory analysis of Latin American politics confirms this assertion. Nevertheless, the successive *coups d'état* must not be seen as a demonstration of the incapacity of Latin American peoples to control their own destiny. On the contrary, the coups, and the violence with which some of their leaders try to maintain themselves in power, are a reaction of the oligarchies, dominated by the metropolis, to the pressure of the people attempting to become people.

autonomy. To counter this effort among a well-intentioned but naïve population, de-mystifying work is necessary to show what the words really stand for: the expression of objective, socio-historical and political categories whose dramatic character in the Third World allows no one to be neutral.

At a time in Brazil when the 'culture of silence' was being exposed for what it is, I began, as a man of the Third World, to elaborate not a mechanical method for adult literacy learning, but an educational theory generated in the womb of the culture of silence itself – a theory which could become in practice not the voice of the culture, but one of the instruments of that still faltering voice.

The thinking developed here is not, of course, free of the influence of other thought. That would be impossible. We have never rejected positive contributions from men of the Third World or of the director societies. But confrontation with our particular world has taught us that any ideas coming from another part of the world cannot simply be transplanted. They must first be submitted to what Professor Guerreiro Ramos in *A Redução Sociologica* calls *sociological reduction*. Unfortunately, such a rigorously scientific attitude is still not widespread in the Third World. Being a world of silence it is still unable – not because of any 'ontological' incapacity, for such a thing does not exist – to assume the posture of one who 'has a voice', who is the subject of his choices, who freely projects his own destiny. Nevertheless, the emerging Third World is rapidly becoming conscious of its plight. It is beginning to understand that the much-publicized need for development cannot be realized under the continuing conditions of silence or of an illusory voice. Under such conditions, only mere modernization is possible.

Thus the fundamental theme of the Third World – implying a difficult but not impossible task for its people – is the conquest of its right to a voice, of the right to pronounce its word. Only then can the word of those who silence it or give it the mere illusion of speaking also become an authentic word. Only by achieving the right to speak its word, the right to be itself, to assume direction of its own destiny, itself, will the Third World create the currently non-existent conditions for those who today silence it to enter into dialogue with it.

As a man of this world, who has already lived some significant, if not excessively traumatic, experiences for having presumed to have a voice in the culture of silence, I have only one desire: that my thinking may coincide historically with the unrest of all those who, whether they live in those cultures which are wholly silenced or in the silent sectors of cultures which prescribe their voice, are struggling to have a voice of their own.

Part One
**The Adult Literacy Process as
Cultural Action for Freedom**

The Adult Literacy Process as Cultural Action for Freedom[1]

Every educational practice implies a concept of man and the world

Experience teaches us not to assume that the obvious is clearly understood. So it is with the truism with which we begin: All educational practice implies a theoretical stance on the educator's part. This stance in turn implies – sometimes more, sometimes less explicitly – an interpretation of man and the world. It could not be otherwise. The process of men's orientation in the world involves not just the association of sense images as it does animals. It involves, above all, thought-language; that is, the possibility of the act of knowing through his praxis, by which man transforms reality. For man, this process of orientation in the world can be understood neither as a purely subjective event, nor as an objective or mechanistic one, but only as an event in which subjectivity and objectivity are united. Orientation in the world, so understood, places the question of the purposes of action at the level of critical perception of reality.

If, for animals, orientation in the world means adaptation to the world, for man it means humanizing the world by transforming it. For animals there is no historical sense, no options or values in their orientation in the world; for man there is both an historical and a value dimension. Men have the sense of 'project', in contrast to the instinctive routines of animals.

The action of men without objectives, whether the objectives are right or wrong, mythical or demythologized, naïve or critical, is not praxis, though it may be orientation in the world. And not being praxis, it is action ignorant both of its own

1. The author gratefully acknowledges the contributions of Loretta Slover, who translated this essay, and João da Veiga Coutinho and Robert Riordan, who assisted in the preparation of the manuscript.

process and of its aim. The interrelation of the awareness of aim and of process is the basis for planning action, which implies methods, objectives and value options.

Teaching adults to read and write must be seen, analysed and understood in this way. The critical analyst will discover in the methods and texts used by educators and students practical value options which betray a philosophy of man, well or poorly outlined, coherent or incoherent. Only someone with a mechanistic mentality, which Marx would call 'grossly materialistic', could reduce adult literacy learning to a purely technical action. Such a naïve approach would be incapable of perceiving that technique itself as an instrument of men in their orientation in the world is not neutral.

We shall try, however, to prove by analysis the self-evidence of our statement. Let us consider the case of primers used as the basic texts for teaching adults to read and write. Let us further propose two distinct types: a poorly done primer and a good one, according to the genre's own criteria. Let us even suppose that the author of the good primer based the selection of its generative words[2] on a prior knowledge of which words have the greatest resonance for the learner (a practice not commonly found, though it does exist).

Doubtlessly, such an author is already far beyond the colleague who composes his primer with words he himself chooses in his own library. Both authors, however, are identical in a fundamental way. In each case they themselves decompose the given generative words and from the syllables create new words.

2. In languages like Portuguese or Spanish, words are composed syllabically. Thus, every non-monosyllabic word is, technically, *generative*, in the sense that other words can be constructed from its decomposed syllables. For a word to be authentically generative, however, certain conditions must be present which will be discussed in a later section of this essay. [At the phonetic level the term *generative word* is properly applicable only with regard to a sound-syllabic reading methodology, while the thematic application is universal. See Sylvia Ashton-Warner's *Teacher* for a different treatment of the concept of generative words at the thematic level.] (*Editor.*)

With these words, in turn, the authors form simple sentences and, little by little, small stories, the so-called reading lessons.

Let us say that the author of the second primer, going one step further, suggests that the teachers who use it initiate discussions about one or another word, sentence or text with their students.

Considering either of these hypothetical cases we may legitimately conclude that there is an implicit concept of man in the primer's method and content, whether it is recognized by the authors or not. This concept can be reconstructed from various angles. We begin with the fact, inherent in the idea and use of the primer, that it is the teacher who chooses the words and proposes them to the learner. Insofar as the primer is the mediating object between the teacher and students, and the students are to be 'filled' with words the teachers have chosen, one can easily detect a first important dimension of the image of man which here begins to emerge. It is the profile of a man whose consciousness is 'spatialized', and must be 'filled' or 'fed' in order to know. This same conception led Sartre, criticizing the notion that 'to know is to eat', in *Situations 1*, to exclaim: '*O philosophie alimentaire!*'

This 'digestive' concept of knowledge, so common in current educational practice, is found very clearly in the primer.[3] Illiterates are considered 'under-nourished', not in the literal sense in which many of them really are, but because they lack the 'bread of the spirit'. Consistent with the concept of knowledge as food, illiteracy is conceived of as a 'poison herb', intoxicating and debilitating persons who cannot read or write. Thus, much is said about the 'eradication' of illiteracy to cure the disease (see my 'La alfabetización de adultos'). In this way, deprived of their character as linguistic signs constitutive of man's thought-language, words are transformed into mere

3. The digestive concept of knowledge is suggested by 'controlled readings'; by classes which consist only in lectures; by the use of memorized dialogues in language learning; by bibliographical notes which indicate not only which chapter, but which lines and words are to be read; by the methods of evaluating the students' progress in learning.

'deposits of vocabulary' – the bread of the spirit which the illiterates are to 'eat' and 'digest'.

This 'nutritionist' view of knowledge perhaps also explains the humanitarian character of certain Latin American adult literacy campaigns. If millions of men are illiterate, 'starving for letters', 'thirsty for words', the word must be *brought* to them to save them from 'hunger' and 'thirst'. The word, according to the naturalistic concept of consciousness implicit in the primer, must be 'deposited', not born of the creative effort of the learners. As understood in this concept, man is a passive being, the object of the process of learning to read and write, and not its subject. As object his task is to 'study' the so-called reading lessons, which in fact are almost completely alienating and alienated, having so little, if anything, to do with the student's socio-cultural reality.[4]

It would be a truly interesting study to analyse the reading texts being used in private or official adult literacy campaigns in rural and urban Latin America. It would not be unusual to find among such texts sentences and readings like the following random samples:[5]

A asa é da ave The wing is of the bird.
Eva viu a uva Eva saw the grape.
O galo canta The cock crows.
O cachorro ladra The dog barks.
Maria gosta dos animais Mary likes animals.
João cuida das arvores John takes care of the trees.

4. There are two noteworthy exceptions among these primers: 1. In Brazil, *Viver e Lutar*, developed by a team of specialists of the Basic Education Movement, sponsored by the National Conference of Bishops. (This reader became the object of controversy after it was banned as subversive by the then governor of Guanabara, Carlos Lacerda, in 1963.) 2. In Chile, the ESPIGA collection, despite some small defects. The collection was organized by Jefatura de Planes Extraordinarios de Educación de Adultos, of the Public Education Ministry.

5. Since at the time this essay was written the writer did not have access to the primers, and was, therefore, vulnerable to recording phrases imprecisely or to confusing the author of one or another primer, it was thought best not to identify the authors or the titles of the books.

O pai de Carlinhos se chama Antonio. Carlinhos é um bom menino, bem comportado e estudioso Charles's father's name is Antonio. Charles is a good, well-behaved and studious boy.

Ada deu o dedo ao urubu? Duvido, Ada deu o dedo a arara. . . .[6]
Se você trabalha com martelo e prego, tenha cuidado para nao furar o dedo. If you hammer a nail, be careful not to smash your finger.[7]

Peter did not know how to read. Peter was ashamed. One day, Peter went to school and registered for a night course. Peter's teacher was very good. Peter knows how to read now. Look at Peter's face. [These lessons are generally illustrated.] Peter is smiling. He is a happy man. He already has a good job. Everyone ought to follow his example.

In saying that Peter is smiling because he knows how to read, that he is happy because he now has a good job, and that he is an example for all to follow, the authors establish a relationship between knowing how to read and getting good jobs which, in fact, cannot be borne out. This naïveté reveals, at least, a failure to perceive the structure not only of illiteracy, but of social phenomena in general. Such an approach may admit that these phenomena exist, but it cannot perceive their relationship to the structure of the society in which they are found. It is as if these phenomena were mythical, above and beyond concrete situations, or the results of the intrinsic inferiority of a certain class of men. Unable to grasp contemporary illiteracy as a typical manifestation of the 'culture of silence', directly related to underdeveloped structures, this approach cannot offer an objective, critical response to the challenge of illiteracy. Merely teaching men to read and write does not work miracles; if there are not enough jobs for men able to work, teaching more men to read and write will not create them.

6. The English here would be nonsensical, as is the Portuguese, the point being the emphasis on the consonant *d*. (*Editor*.)
7. The author may even have added here, '. . . If, however, this should happen, apply a little mercurochrome.'

One of these readers presents among its lessons the following two texts on consecutive pages without relating them. The first is about 1 May, the Labour Day holiday, on which workers commemorate their struggles. It does not say how or where these are commemorated, or what the nature of the historical conflict was. The main theme of the second lesson is *holidays*. It says that 'on these days people ought to go to the beach to swim and sunbathe. . . .' Therefore, if 1 May is a holiday, and if on holidays people should go to the beach, the conclusion is that the workers should go swimming on Labour Day, instead of meeting with their unions in the public squares to discuss their problems.

Analysis of these texts reveals, then, a simplistic vision of men, of their world, of the relationship between the two, and of the literacy process which unfolds in that world.

A asa é da ave, Eva viu a uva, o galo canta, and *o cachorro ladra* are linguistic contexts which, when mechanically memorized and repeated, are deprived of their authentic dimension as thought-language in dynamic interplay with reality. Thus impoverished, they are not authentic expressions of the world.

Their authors do not recognize in the poor classes the ability to know and even create the texts which would express their own thought-language at the level of their perception of the world. The authors repeat with the texts what they do with the words, i.e., they introduce them into the learners' consciousness as if it were empty space – once more, the 'digestive' concept of knowledge.

Still more, the a-structural perception of illiteracy revealed in these texts exposes the other false view of illiterates as marginal men.[8] Those who consider them marginal must, nevertheless,

8. The Portuguese word here translated as *marginal man* is *marginado*. This has a passive sense: he who has been made marginal, or sent outside society; as well as the sense of a state of existence on the fringe of society. (*Translator*.)

recognize the existence of a reality to which they are marginal – not only physical space, but historical, social, cultural, and economic realities – i.e. the structural dimension of reality. In this way, illiterates have to be recognized as beings 'outside of', 'marginal to' something, since it is impossible to be marginal to nothing. But being 'outside of' or 'marginal to' necessarily implies a movement of the one said to be marginal from the centre, where he was, to the periphery. This movement, which is an action, presupposes in turn not only an agent but also his reasons. Admitting the existence of men 'outside of' or 'marginal to' structural reality, it seems legitimate to ask: Who is the author of this movement from the centre of the structure to its margin? Do so-called marginal men, among them the illiterates, make the decision to move out to the periphery of society? If so, marginality is an option with all that it involves: hunger, sickness, rickets, pain, mental deficiencies, living death, crime, promiscuity, despair, the impossibility of being. In fact, however, it is difficult to accept that 40 per cent of Brazil's population, almost 90 per cent of Haiti's, 60 per cent of Bolivia's, about 40 per cent of Peru's, more than 30 per cent of Mexico's and Venezuela's, and about 70 per cent of Guatemala's would have made the tragic *choice* of their own marginality as illiterates (see UNESCO's *La Situación Educativa en América Latina*). If, then, marginality is not by choice, marginal man has been expelled from and kept outside of the social system and is therefore the object of violence.

In fact, however, the social structure as a whole does not 'expel', nor is marginal man a 'being outside of'. He is, on the contrary, a 'being inside of', within the social structure, and in a dependent relationship to those whom we falsely call autonomous beings, inauthentic beings-for-themselves.

A less rigorous approach, one more simplistic, less critical, more technicist, would say that it was unnecessary to reflect about what it would consider unimportant questions such as illiteracy and teaching adults to read and write. Such an approach might even add that the discussion of the concept of marginality is an unnecessary academic exercise. In fact, however, it is not so. In accepting the illiterate as a person who exists on the fringe of society, we are led to view him as a sort of 'sick man', for whom literacy would be the 'medicine' to cure him, enabling him to 'return' to the 'healthy' structure from which he has become separated. Educators would be benevolent counsellors, scouring the outskirts of the city for the stubborn illiterates, runaways from the good life, to restore them to the forsaken bosom of happiness by giving them the gift of the word.

In the light of such a concept – unfortunately, all too widespread – literacy programmes can never be efforts toward freedom; they will never question the very reality which deprives men of the right to speak up – not only illiterates, but all those who are treated as objects in a dependent relationship. These men, illiterate or not, are, in fact, not marginal. What we said before bears repeating: they are not 'beings outside of'; they are 'beings for another'. Therefore the solution to their problem is not to become 'beings inside of', but men freeing themselves; for, in reality, they are not marginal to the structure, but oppressed men within it. Alienated men, they cannot overcome their dependency by 'incorporation' into the very structure responsible for their dependency. There is no other road to humanization – theirs as well as everyone else's – but authentic transformation of the dehumanizing structure.

From this last point of view, the illiterate is no longer a person living on the fringe of society, a marginal man, but rather a representative of the dominated strata of society, in conscious or unconscious opposition to those who, in the same structure, treat him as a thing. Thus, also, teaching men to read and write is no longer an inconsequential matter of *ba*, *be*, *bi*, *bo*, *bu*, of memorizing an alienated word, but a difficult apprenticeship in naming the world.

In the first hypothesis, interpreting illiterates as men marginal to society, the literacy process reinforces the mythification of reality by keeping it opaque and by dulling the 'empty consciousness' of the learner with innumerable alienating words and phrases. By contrast, in the second hypothesis – interpreting illiterates as men oppressed within the system – the literacy process, as cultural action for freedom, is an act of knowing in which the learner assumes the role of knowing subject in dialogue with the educator. For this very reason, it is a courageous endeavour to demythologize reality, a process through which men who had previously been submerged in reality begin to emerge in order to re-insert themselves into it with critical awareness.

Therefore the educator must strive for an ever greater clarity as to what, at times without his conscious knowledge, illumines the path of his action. Only in this way will he truly be able to assume the role of one of the subjects of this action and remain consistent in the process.

The adult literacy process as an act of knowing

To be an act of knowing the adult literacy process demands among teachers and students a relationship of authentic dialogue. True dialogue unites subjects together in the cognition of a knowable object which mediates between them.

If learning to read and write is to constitute an act of knowing, the learners must assume from the beginning the role of creative subjects. It is not a matter of memorizing and repeating given syllables, words and phrases, but rather of reflecting critically on the process of reading and writing itself, and on the profound significance of language.

Insofar as language is impossible without thought, and language and thought are impossible without the world to which they refer, the human word is more than mere vocabulary – it is word-and-action. The cognitive dimensions of the literacy process must include the relationships of men with their world. These relationships are the source of the dialectic between the products men achieve in transforming the world and the conditioning which these products in turn exercise on men.

Learning to read and write ought to be an opportunity for men to know what *speaking the word* really means: a human act implying reflection and action. As such it is a primordial human right and not the privilege of a few, as I point out in my 'La alfabetazación de adultos'. Speaking the word is not a true act if it is not at the same time associated with the right of self-expression and world-expression, of creating and re-creating, of deciding and choosing and ultimately participating in society's historical process.

In the culture of silence the masses are 'mute', that is, they are prohibited from creatively taking part in the transformations of their society and therefore prohibited from being. Even if they can occasionally read and write because they were 'taught' in humanitarian – but not humanist – literacy campaigns, they are nevertheless alienated from the power responsible for their silence.

Illiterates know they are concrete men. They know that they do things. What they do not know in the culture of silence – in which they are ambiguous, dual beings – is that men's actions as such are transforming, creative, and re-creative. Overcome by the myths of this culture, including the myth of their own 'natural inferiority', they do not know that *their* action upon the world is also transforming. Prevented from having a 'structural perception' of the facts involving them, they do not know that they cannot 'have a voice', that is, that they cannot exercise the right to participate consciously in the socio-historical transformation of their society, because their work does not belong to them.

It could be said (and I would agree) that it is not possible to recognize all this apart from praxis, that is, apart from reflection and action, and that to attempt it would be pure idealism. But it is also true that action upon an object must be critically analysed in order to understand both the object itself and the understanding one has of it. The act of knowing involves a dialectical movement which goes from action to reflection and from reflection upon action to a new action. For the learner to know what he did not know before, he must engage in an authentic process of abstraction by means of which he can reflect on the action-object whole, or, more generally, on forms of orientation in the world. In this process of abstraction, situations representative of how the learner orients himself in the world are proposed to him as the objects of his critique.

As an event calling forth the critical reflection of both the learners and educators, the literacy process must relate *speaking the word* to *transforming reality*, and to man's role in this transformation. Perceiving the significance of that relationship is indispensable for those learning to read and write if we are really committed to liberation. Such a perception will lead the learners to recognize a much greater right than that of being literate. They will ultimately recognize that, as men, they have the right to have a voice.

On the other hand, as an act of knowing, learning to read and write presupposes not only a theory of knowing but a method which corresponds to the theory.

We recognize the indisputable unity between subjectivity and objectivity in the act of knowing. Reality is never just simply the objective datum, the concrete fact, but is also men's perception of it. Once again, this is not a subjectivistic or idealistic affirmation, as it might seem. On the contrary, subjectivism and idealism come into play when the subjective–objective unity is broken.[9]

The adult literacy process as an act of knowing implies the existence of two interrelated contexts. One is the context of authentic dialogue between learners and educators as equally knowing subjects. This is what schools should be – the theoreti-

9. 'There are two ways to fall into idealism: the one consists of dissolving the real in subjectivity; the other in denying all real subjectivity in the interests of objectivity,' says Sartre in *Search for a Method*.

cal context of dialogue. The second is the real, concrete context of facts, the social reality in which men exist. (See Kosik in *Dialectica de lo Concreto*.)

In the theoretical context of dialogue, the facts presented by the real or concrete context are critically analysed. This analysis involves the exercise of abstraction, through which, by means of representations of concrete reality, we seek knowledge of that reality. The instrument for this abstraction in our methodology is codification,[10] or representation of the existential situations of the learners.

Codification, on the one hand, mediates between the concrete and theoretical contexts (of reality). On the other hand, as knowable object, it mediates between the knowing subjects, educators and learners, who seek in dialogue to unveil the 'action-object wholes'.

This type of linguistic discourse must be 'read' by anyone who tries to interpret it, even when purely pictorial. As such, it presents what Chomsky calls 'surface structure' and 'deep structure'.

The 'surface structure' of codification makes the 'action-object whole' explicit in a purely taxonomic form. The first stage of decodification[11] – or reading – is descriptive. At this stage, the 'readers' – or decodifiers – focus on the relationship between the categories constituting the codification. This preliminary focus on the surface structure is followed by problematizing the codified situation. This leads the learner to the second and fundamental stage of decodification, the com-

10. Codification refers alternatively to the imaging, or the image itself of some significant aspect of the learner's concrete reality (of a slum dwelling, for example). As such, it becomes both the object of the teacher-learner dialogue and the context for the introduction of the generative word. (*Editor*.)

11. Decodification refers to a process of description and interpretation, whether of printed words, pictures or other 'codifications'. As such, decodification and decodifying are distinct from the process of decoding, or word-recognition. (*Editor*.)

prehension of the codification's 'deep structure'. By understanding the codification's 'deep structure' the learner can then understand the dialectic which exists between the categories presented in the 'surface structure', as well as the unity between the 'surface' and 'deep' structures.

In our method, the codification initially takes the form of a photograph or sketch which represents a real existent, or an existent constructed by the learners. When this representation is projected as a slide, the learners effect an operation basic to the act of knowing: they gain distance from the knowable object. This experience of distance is undergone as well by the educators, so that educators and learners together can reflect critically on the knowable object which mediates between them. The aim of decodification is to arrive at the critical level of knowing, beginning with the learner's experience of the situation in the 'real context'.

Whereas the codified representation is the knowable object mediating between knowing subjects, decodification – dissolving the codification into its constituent elements – is the operation by which the knowing subjects perceive relationships between the codification's elements and other facts presented by the real context – relationships which were formerly unperceived. Codification represents a given dimension of reality as individuals live it, and this dimension is proposed for their analysis in a context other than that in which they live it. Codification thus transforms what was a way of life in the real context into 'objectum' in the theoretical context. The learners, rather than receive information about this or that fact, analyse aspects of their own existential experience represented in the codification.

Existential experience is a whole. In illuminating one of its angles and perceiving the interrelation between that angle and others, the learners tend to replace a fragmented vision of reality with a total vision. From the point of view of a theory of knowledge, this means that the dynamic between codification of existential situations and decodification involves the learners in a constant reconstruction of their former 'ad-miration' of reality.

I do not use the concept 'ad-miration' here in the usual way, or in its ethical or aesthetic sense, but with a special philosophical connotation.

To 'ad-mire' is to objectify the 'not-I'. It is a dialectical operation which characterizes man as man, differentiating between him and the animal. It is directly associated with the creative dimension of his language. To 'ad-mire' implies that man stands over against his 'not-I' in order to understand it. For this reason, there is no act of knowing without 'ad-miration' of the object to be known. If the act of knowing is a dynamic act – and no knowledge is ever complete – then in order to know, man not only 'ad-mires' the object, but must always be 're-ad-miring' his former 'ad-miration'. When we 're-ad-mire' our former 'ad-miration' (always an 'ad-miration' *of*) we are simultaneously 'ad-miring' the act of 'ad-miring' and the object 'ad-mired', so that we can overcome the errors we made in our former 'ad-miration'. This 're-ad-miration' leads us to a perception of an anterior perception.

In the process of decodifying representations of their existential situations and perceiving former perceptions, the learners gradually, hesitatingly and timorously place in doubt the opinion they held of reality and replace it with a more and more critical knowledge.

Let us suppose that we were to present to groups from among the dominated classes codifications which portray their imitation of the dominators' cultural models – a natural tendency of the oppressed consciousness at a given moment.[12] The dominated persons would perhaps, in self-defence, deny the truth of the codification. As they deepened their analysis, however, they

12. Re the oppressed consciousness, see: Frantz Fanon's *The Wretched of the Earth*; Albert Memmi's *Colonizer and the Colonized*; and my *Pedagogy of the Oppressed*.

would begin to perceive that their apparent imitation of the dominators' models is a result of their interiorization of these models and, above all, of the myths about the 'superiority' of the dominant classes which cause the dominated to feel inferior. What in fact is pure interiorization appears in a naïve analysis to be imitation. Basically, as I point out in *Pedogagy of the Oppressed*, when the dominated classes reproduce the dominators' style of life, it is because the dominators live 'within' the dominated. The dominated can eject the dominators only by getting distance from them and objectifying them. Only then can they recognize them as their antithesis, as Fanon says.

To the extent, however, that interiorization of the dominators' values is not only an individual phenomenon, but a social and cultural one, ejection must be achieved by a type of cultural action in which culture negates culture. That is, culture, as an interiorized product which in turn conditions men's subsequent acts, must become the object of men's knowledge so that they can perceive its conditioning power. Cultural action occurs at the level of superstructure. It can only be understood by what Althusser calls 'the dialectic of overdetermination' (see also my *Annual Report*). This analytic tool prevents us from falling into mechanistic explanations or, what is worse, mechanistic action. An understanding of it precludes surprise that cultural myths remain after the infrastructure is transformed, even by revolution.

When the creation of a new culture is appropriate but impeded by interiorized cultural 'residue', this residue, the myths, must be expelled by means of culture. Cultural action and cultural revolution, at different stages, constitute the modes of this expulsion.

The learners must discover the reasons behind many of their attitudes toward cultural reality and thus confront cultural reality in a new way. 'Re-ad-miration' of their former 'ad-miration' is necessary in order to bring this about. The learners' capacity for critical knowing – well beyond mere opinion – is established in the process of unveiling their relationships with the historical-cultural world *in* and *with* which they exist.

We do not mean to suggest that critical knowledge of man-world relationships arises as a verbal knowledge outside of praxis. Praxis is involved in the concrete situations which are codified for critical analysis. To analyse the codification in its 'deep structure' is, for this very reason, to reconstruct the former praxis and to become capable of a new and different praxis. The relationship between the *theoretical context*, in which codified representations of objective facts are analysed, and the *concrete context*, where these facts occur, has to be made real.

Such education must have the character of commitment. It implies a movement from the concrete context which provides objective facts, to the theoretical context where these facts are analysed in depth, and back to the concrete context where men experiment with new forms of praxis.

It might seem as if some of our statements defend the principle that, whatever the level of the learners, they ought to reconstruct the process of human knowing in absolute terms. In fact, when we consider adult literacy learning or education in general as an act of knowing, we are advocating a synthesis between the educator's maximally systematized knowing and the learners' minimally systematized knowing – a synthesis achieved in dialogue. The educator's role is to propose problems about the codified existential situations in order to help the learners arrive at an increasingly critical view of their reality. The educator's responsibility as conceived by this philosophy is thus greater in every way than that of his colleague whose duty is to transmit information which the learners memorize. Such an educator can simply repeat what he has read, and often misunderstood, since education for him does not mean an act of knowing.

The first type of educator, on the contrary, is a knowing subject, face to face with other knowing subjects. He can never be a mere memorizer, but a person constantly readjusting his knowledge, who calls forth knowledge from his students. For him, education is a pedagogy of knowing. The educator whose approach is mere memorization is anti-dialogic; his act of transmitting knowledge is unalterable. In contrast, for the educator who experiences the act of knowing together with his students, dialogue is the seal of the act of knowing. He is aware, however, that not all dialogue is in itself the mark of a relationship of true knowledge.

Socratic intellectualism – which mistook the definition of the concept for knowledge of the thing defined and this knowledge as virtue – did not constitute a true pedagogy of knowing, even though it was dialogic. Plato's theory of dialogue failed to go beyond the Socratic theory of the definition as knowledge, even though for Plato one of the necessary conditions for knowing was that man be capable of a *prise de conscience*, and though the passage from *doxa* to *logos* was indispensable for man to achieve truth. For Plato, the *prise de conscience* did not refer to what man knew or did not know or knew badly about his dialectical relationship with the world; it was concerned rather with what man once knew and forgot at birth. To know was to remember or recollect forgotten knowledge. The apprehension of both *doxa* and *logos*, and the overcoming of *doxa* by *logos*, occurred not in the man-world relationship, but in the effort to remember or rediscover a forgotten *logos*.

For dialogue to be a method of true knowledge, the knowing subjects must approach reality scientifically in order to seek the dialectical connections which explain the form of reality. Thus, to know is not to remember something previously known and now forgotten. Nor can *doxa* be overcome by *logos* apart from the dialectical relationship of man with his world, apart from man's reflective action upon the world.

To be an act of knowing, then, the adult literacy process must engage the learners in the constant problematizing of their existential situations. This problematizing employs 'generative words' chosen by specialized educators in a preliminary investigation of what we call the 'minimal linguistic universe' of the future learners. The words are chosen firstly for their pragmatic value, that is, as linguistic signs which command a common understanding in a region or area of the same city or country (in the United States, for instance, the word *soul* has a special significance in black areas which it does not have among whites), and secondly for their phonetic difficulties which will gradually be presented to those learning to read and write. Finally, it is important that the first generative word be tri-syllabic. When it is divided into its syllables, each one constituting a syllabic family, the learners can experiment with various syllabic combinations even at first sight of the word.

Having chosen seventeen generative words,[13] the next step is to codify seventeen existential situations familiar to the learners. The generative words are then worked into the situations one by one in the order of their increasing phonetic difficulty. As we have already emphasized, these codifications are knowable objects which mediate between the knowing subjects, educator-learners, learner-educators. Their act of knowing is elaborated in the *circulo de cultura* (cultural discussion group) which functions as the theoretical context.

In Brazil, before analysing the learners' existential situations and the generative words contained in them, we proposed the codified theme of man–world relationships in general, as I describe in *Educação como Práctica da Libertade*. In Chile, at the suggestion of Chilean educators, this important dimension was discussed concurrently with learning to read and write. What is important is that the person learning words be concomitantly engaged in a critical analysis of the social framework in which men exist. For example, the word *favela* (slum) in Rio de Janeiro, Brazil, and the word *callampa* in Chile, represent, each with its own nuances, the same social, economic, and cul-

13. We observed in Brazil and Spanish America, especially Chile, that no more than seventeen words were necessary for teaching adults to read and write syllabic languages like Portuguese and Spanish.

tural reality of the vast numbers of slum dwellers in those countries. If *favela* and *callampa* are used as generative words for the people of Brazilian and Chilean slums, the codifications will have to represent slum situations.

There are many people who consider slum dwellers marginal, intrinsically wicked and inferior. To such people we recommend the profitable experience of discussing the slum situation with slum dwellers themselves. As some of these critics are often simply mistaken, it is possible that they may rectify their mythical clichés and assume a more scientific attitude. They may avoid saying that the illiteracy, alcoholism and crime of the slums, its sickness, infant mortality, learning deficiencies and poor hygiene reveal the 'inferior nature' of its inhabitants. They may even end up realizing that if intrinsic evil exists it is part of the structures, and that it is the structures which need to be transformed.

It should be pointed out that the Third World as a whole, and more in some parts than in others, suffers from the same misunderstanding from certain sectors of the so-called metropolitan societies. They see the Third World as the incarnation of evil, the primitive, the devil, sin and sloth – in sum, as historically unviable without the director societies. Such a manichean attitude is at the source of the impulse to 'save' the 'demon-possessed' Third World, 'educating' it and 'correcting its thinking' according to the director societies' own criteria.

The expansionist interests of the director societies are implicit in such notions. These societies can never relate to the Third World as partners, since partnership presupposes equals, no matter how different the equal parties may be, and can never be established between parties antagonistic to each other.

Thus, 'salvation' of the Third World by the director societies can only mean its domination, whereas in its legitimate aspiration to independence lies its utopian vision: to save the director societies in the very act of freeing itself.

In this sense the pedagogy which we defend, conceived in a

significant area of the Third World, is itself a utopian pedagogy. By this very fact it is full of hope, for to be utopian is not to be merely idealistic or impractical but rather to engage in denunciation and annunciation. Our pedagogy cannot do without a vision of man and of the world. It formulates a scientific humanist conception which finds its expression in a dialogical praxis in which the teachers and learners together, in the act of analysing a dehumanizing reality, denounce it while announcing its transformation in the name of the liberation of man.

For this very reason, denunciation and annunciation in this utopian pedagogy are not meant to be empty words, but an historic commitment. Denunciation of a dehumanizing situation today increasingly demands precise scientific understanding of that situation. Likewise, the annunciation of its transformation increasingly requires a theory of transforming action. However, neither act by itself implies the transformation of the denounced reality or the establishment of that which is announced. Rather, as a moment in an historical process, the announced reality is already present in the act of denunciation and annunciation.[14]

That is why the utopian character of our educational theory and practice is as permanent as education itself which, for us, is cultural action. Its thrust toward denunciation and annunciation cannot be exhausted when the reality denounced today cedes its place tomorrow to the reality previously announced in the denunciation. When education is no longer utopian, that is, when it no longer embodies the dramatic unity of denunciation and annunciation, it is either because the future has no more meaning for men, or because men are afraid to risk living the future as creative overcoming of the present, which has become old.

The more likely explanation is generally the latter. That is why some people today study all the possibilities which the future contains, in order to 'domesticate' it and keep it in line

14. Re the utopian dimension of denunciation and proclamation, see Leszek Kolakowski, *Toward a Marxist Humanism*.

with the present, which is what they intend to maintain. If there is any anguish in director societies hidden beneath the cover of their cold technology, it springs from their desperate determination that their metropolitan status be preserved in the future. Among the things which the Third World may learn from the metropolitan societies this is fundamental: not to reproduce those societies when its current utopia becomes actual fact.

When we defend such a conception of education – realistic precisely to the extent that it is utopian – that is, to the extent that it denounces what in fact is, and finds therefore between denunciation and its realization the time of its praxis – we are attempting to formulate a type of education which corresponds to the specifically human mode of being, which is historical.

There is no annunciation without denunciation, just as every denunciation generates annunciation. Without the latter, hope is impossible. In an authentic utopian vision, however, hoping does not mean folding one's arms and waiting. Waiting is only possible when, filled with hope, one seeks through reflective action to achieve that 'announced' future which is being born within the denunciation.

That is why there is no genuine hope in those who intend to make the future repeat their present, nor in those who see the future as something predetermined. Both have a 'domesticated' notion of history: the former because they want to stop time; the latter because they are certain about a future they already 'know'. Utopian hope, on the contrary, is engagement full of risk. That is why the dominators, who merely denounce those who denounce them, and who have nothing to announce but the preservation of the *status quo*, can never be utopian nor, for that matter, prophetic. [15]

15. 'The Right, as a conservative force, needs no utopia; its essence is the affirmation of existing conditions – a fact and not a utopia – or else the desire to revert to a state which was once an accomplished fact. The Right strives to idealize actual conditions, not to change them. What it needs is fraud not utopia,' says Kolakowski.

A utopian pedagogy of denunciation and annunciation such as ours will have to be an act of knowing the denounced reality at the level of alphabetization and post-alphabetization, which both constitute cultural action. That is why there is such emphasis on the continual problematization of the learners' existential situations as represented in the codified images. The longer the problematization proceeds, and the more the subjects enter into the 'essence' of the problematized object, the more they are able to unveil this 'essence'. The more they unveil it, the more their awakening consciousness deepens, thus leading to the 'conscientization' of the situation by the poor classes. Their critical self-insertion into reality, that is, their conscientization, makes the transformation of their state of apathy into the utopian state of denunciation and annunciation a viable project.

One must not think, however, that learning to read and write precedes 'conscientization', or vice-versa. Conscientization occurs simultaneously with the literacy or post-literacy process. It must be so. In our educational method, the word is not something static or disconnected from men's existential experience but a dimension of their thought-language about the world. That is why, when they participate critically in analysing the first generative words linked with their existential experience; when they focus on the syllabic families which result from that analysis; when they perceive the mechanism of the syllabic combinations of their language, the learners finally discover, in the various possibilities of combination, their own words. Little by little, as these possibilities multiply, the learners, through mastery of new generative words, expand both their vocabulary and their capacity for expression by the development of their creative imagination.[16]

16. 'We have observed that the study of the creative aspect of language use develops the assumption that linguistic and mental process are virtually identical, language providing the primary means for free expansion of thought and feeling, as well as for the functioning of creative imagination,' writes Noam Chomsky in *Cartesian Linguistics*.

In some areas in Chile undergoing agrarian reform, the peasants participating in the literacy programmes wrote words with their tools on the dirt roads where they were working. They composed the words from the syllabic combinations they were learning. 'These men are sowers of the word,' said Maria Edi Ferreira, a sociologist from the Santiago team working in the Institute of Training and Research in Agrarian Reform. Indeed, they were not only sowing words, but discussing ideas, and coming to understand their role in the world better and better.

We asked one of these 'sowers of words', finishing the first level of literacy classes, why he hadn't learned to read and write before the agrarian reform.

'Before the agrarian reform, my friend,' he said, 'I didn't even think. Neither did my friends.'

'Why?' we asked.

'Because it wasn't possible. We lived under orders. We only had to carry out orders. We had nothing to say,' he replied emphatically.

The simple answer of this peasant is a very clear analysis of 'the culture of silence'. In 'the culture of silence', to exist is only to live. The body carries out orders from above. Thinking is difficult, speaking the word, forbidden.

'When all this land belonged to one *latifundio*,' said another man in the same conversation, 'there was no reason to read and write. We weren't responsible for anything. The boss gave the orders and we obeyed. Why read and write? Now it's a different story. Take me, for example. In the *asentamiento*,[17]

17. After the disappropriation of lands in the agrarian reform in Chile, the peasants who were salaried workers on the large *latifundia* become 'settlers' (*asentados*) during a three-year period in which they receive varied assistance from the government through the Agrarian Reform Corporation. This period of 'settlement' (*asentamiento*) precedes that of assigning lands to the peasants. This policy is now changing. The phase of 'settlement' of the lands is being abolished, in favour of an immediate distribution of lands to the peasants. The Agrarian Reform Corporation will continue, nevertheless, to aid the peasants.

I am responsible not only for my work like all the other men, but also for tool repairs. When I started I couldn't read, but I soon realized that I needed to read and write. You can't imagine what it was like to go to Santiago to buy parts. I couldn't get orientated. I was afraid of everything – afraid of the big city, of buying the wrong thing, of being cheated. Now it's all different.'

Observe how precisely this peasant described his former experience as an illiterate: his mistrust, his magical (though logical) fear of the world, his timidity. And observe the sense of security with which he repeats, 'Now it's all different.'

'What did you feel, my friend,' we asked another 'sower of words' on a different occasion, 'when you were able to write and read your first word?'

'I was happy because I discovered I could make words speak,' he replied.

Dario Salas reports, 'In our conversations with peasants we were struck by the images they used to express their interest and satisfaction about becoming literate. For example, "Before we were blind, now the veil has fallen from our eyes": "I came only to learn how to sign my name. I never believed I would be able to read, too, at my age"; "Before, letters seemed like little puppets. Today they say something to me, and I can make them talk."

'It is touching,' continues Salas, 'to observe the delight of the peasants as the world of words opens to them. Sometimes they would say, "We're so tired our heads ache, but we don't want to leave here without learning to read and write."'[18]

The following words were taped during research on 'genera-

18. Dario Salas refers here to one of the best adult education programmes organized by the Agrarian Reform Corporation in Chile, in strict collaboration with the Ministry of Education and ICIRA (Agrarian Reform, Training and Research Institute). Fifty peasants receive boarding and instruction scholarships for a month. The courses centre on discussions of the local, regional and national situations.

tive themes'.[19] They are an illiterate's decodification of a codified existential situation.

'You see a house there, sad, as if it were abandoned. When you see a house with a child in it, it seems happier. It gives more joy and peace to people passing by. The father of the family arrives home from work exhausted, worried, bitter, and his little boy comes to meet him with a big hug, because a little boy is not stiff like a big person. The father already begins to be happier just from seeing his children. Then he really enjoys himself. He is moved by his son's wanting to please him. The father becomes more peaceful, and forgets his problems.'

Note once again the simplicity of expression, both profound and elegant, in the peasant's language. These are the people considered absolutely ignorant by the proponents of the 'digestive' concept of literacy.

In 1968, an Uruguayan team published a small book, *You Live as You Can* (*Se Vive como se Puede*), whose contents are taken from the tape recordings of literacy classes for urban dwellers. Its first edition of three thousand copies was sold out in Montevideo in fifteen days, as was the second edition. The following is an excerpt from this book.

The colour of water

Water? Water? What is water used for?

'Yes, yes, we saw it (in the picture).'

'Oh, my native village, so far away...'

'Do you remember that village?'

'The stream where I grew up, called Dead Friar ... you know, I grew up there, a childhood moving from one place to another ... the colour of the water brings back good memories, beautiful memories.'

'What is the water used for?'

'It is used for washing. We used it to wash clothes, and the animals

19. An analysis of the objectives and methodology of the investigation of generative themes lies outside the scope of this essay, but is dealt with in my *Pedagogy of the Oppressed*.

in the fields used to go there to drink, and we washed ourselves there, too.'

'Did you also use the water for drinking?'

'Yes, when we were at the stream and had no other water to drink, we drank from the stream. I remember once in 1945 a plague of locusts came from somewhere, and we had to fish them out of the water ... I was small, but I remember taking out the locusts like this, with my two hands – and I had no others. And I remember how hot the water was when there was a drought and the stream was almost dry ... the water was dirty, muddy and hot, with all kinds of things in it. But we had to drink it or die of thirst.'

The whole book is like this, pleasant in style, with great strength of expression of the world of its authors, those anonymous people, 'sowers of words', seeking to emerge from 'the culture of silence'.

Yes, these ought to be the reading texts for people learning to read and write, and not 'Eva saw the grape', 'The bird's wing', 'If you hammer a nail, be careful not to hit your fingers.' Intellectualist prejudices and above all class prejudices are responsible for the naïve and unfounded notions that the people cannot write their own texts, or that a tape of their conversations is valueless since their conversations are impoverished of meaning. Comparing what the 'sowers of words' said in the above references with what is generally written by specialist authors of reading lessons, we are convinced that only someone with very pronounced lack of taste or a lamentable scientific incompetency would choose the specialists' texts.

Imagine a book written entirely in this simple, poetic, free, language of the people, a book on which interdisciplinary teams would collaborate in the spirit of true dialogue. The role of the teams would be to elaborate specialized sections of the book in problematic terms. For example, a section on linguistics would deal simply, though not simplistically, with questions fundamental to the learners' critical understanding of language. Let me emphasize again that since one of the important aspects of adult literacy work is the development of the capacity for expression, the section on linguistics would present themes for the learners to discuss, ranging from the increase of vocabulary to questions about communication – including the study of synonyms and antonyms, with its analysis of words in the linguistic context, and the use of metaphor, of which the people are such masters. Another section might provide the tools for a sociological analysis of the content of the texts.

These texts would not, of course, be used for mere mechanical reading, which leaves the readers without any understanding of what is real. Consistent with the nature of this pedagogy, they would become the object of analysis in reading seminars.

Add to all this the great stimulus it would be for those learning to read and write, as well as for students on more advanced levels, to know that they were reading and discussing the work of their own companions. . . .

To undertake such a work, it is necessary to have faith in the people, solidarity with them. It is necessary to be utopian, in the sense in which we have used the word.

Part Two
Cultural Action and Conscientization

Cultural Action and Conscientization[1]

Existence *in* and *with* the world

It is appropriate at this point to make an explicit and systematic analysis of the concept of conscientization.[2]

The starting point for such an analysis must be a critical comprehension of man as a being who exists *in* and *with* the world. Since the basic condition for 'conscientization' is that its agent must be a subject (that is a conscious being), 'conscientization', like education, is specifically and exclusively a human process. It is as conscious beings that men are not only *in* the world, but *with* the world, together with other men. Only men, as 'open' beings, are able to achieve the complex operation of simultaneously transforming the world by their action and grasping and expressing the world's reality in their creative language.

Men can fulfil the necessary condition of being *with* the world because they are able to gain objective distance from it. Without this objectification, whereby man also objectifies himself, man would be limited to being *in* the world, lacking both self-knowledge and knowledge of the world,

Unlike men, animals are simply *in* the world, incapable of objectifying either themselves or the world. They live a life without time, properly speaking, submerged in life with no

1. This is part 3 of Paulo Freire's 'Conscientization: Cultural Action for Freedom', the first two parts of which appeared in the May 1970 issue of the *Harvard Educational Review*. Translated by Loretta Slover. Copyright © 1970 by the Center for the Study of Development and Social Change, 1430 Massachusetts Avenue, Cambridge, Massachusetts 02138.

2. Conscientization refers to the process in which men, not as recipients, but as knowing subjects, achieve a deepening awareness both of the sociocultural reality which shapes their lives and of their capacity to transform that reality. See Part One. (*Editor.*)

possibility of emerging from it, adjusted and adhering to reality. Men, on the contrary, who can sever this adherence and transcend mere being in the world, add to the life which they have the existence which they make. To exist is thus a mode of life which is proper to the being who is capable of transforming, of producing, of deciding, of creating, and of communicating himself.

Whereas the being which merely lives is not capable of reflecting upon itself and knowing itself living *in* the world, the existent subject reflects upon his life within the very domain of existence, and questions his relationship with the world. His domain of existence is the domain of work, of history, of culture, of values – the domain in which men experience the dialectic between determinism and freedom.

If they did not sever their adherence to the world and emerge from it as consciousness constituted in the 'ad-miration' of the world as its object, men would be merely determinate beings, and it would be impossible to think in terms of their liberation. Only beings who can reflect upon the fact that they are determined are capable of freeing themselves. Their reflectiveness results not just in a vague and uncommitted awareness, but in the exercise of a profoundly transforming action upon the determining reality. *Consciousness of* and *action upon* reality are, therefore, inseparable constituents of the transforming act by which men become beings of relation.[3] By their characteristic reflection, intentionality, temporality and 'transcendence',[4] men's consciousness and action are distinct from the mere *contacts* of animals with the world. The animals' contacts are a-critical; they do not go beyond the association of sensory images through experience. They are singular and not plural.

3. *Re* the distinction between men's relationships and the contacts of animals, see Paulo Freire, *Educação como Prática da Liberdade.*
4. Transcendence in this context signifies the capacity of human consciousness to surpass the limitations of the objective configuration. Without this 'transcendental intentionality' consciousness of what exists beyond limitations would be impossible. For example I am aware of how the table at which I write limits me only because I can transcend and focus my attention upon its limits.

Animals do not elaborate goals; they exist at the level of immersion and are thus a-temporal.

Engagement and objective distance, understanding reality as object, understanding the significance of men's action upon objective reality, creative communication about the object by means of language, plurality of responses to a single challenge – these varied dimensions testify to the existence of critical reflection in men's relationships with the world. Consciousness is constituted in the dialectic of man's objectification of and action upon the world. However, consciousness is never a mere reflection of, but a reflection upon, material reality.[5]

If it is true that consciousness is impossible without the world which constitutes it, it is equally true that this world is impossible if the world itself in constituting consciousness does not become an object of its critical reflection. Thus, since it negates men, mechanistic objectivism is incapable of explaining men and the world, as is solipsistic idealism since it negates the world.

For mechanistic objectivism, consciousness is merely a 'copy' of objective reality. For solipsism, the world is reduced to a capricious creation of consciousness. In the first case, consciousness would be unable to transcend its conditioning by reality; in the second, insofar as it 'creates' reality, it is *a priori* to reality. In either case man is not engaged in transforming reality. That would be impossible in objectivistic terms, because for objectivism, consciousness, the replica or 'copy' of reality, is the object of reality, and reality would then be transformed by itself.[6] The solipsistic view is equally incompatible

5. '"Man, a reasoning animal", said Aristotle.

"Man, a reflective animal", let us say more exactly today, putting the accent on the evolutionary characteristics of a quality which signifies the passage from a still diffuse consciousness to one sufficiently well centred to be capable of coinciding with itself. Man is not only "a being who knows" but "a being who knows he knows". Possessing *consciousness raised to the power of two*.... Do we sufficiently feel the radical nature of the difference?' writes Pierre Teilhard de Chardin in *The Appearance of Man*.

6. Marx rejects the transformation of reality by itself in one of his 'Theses on Feuerbach' (3); see *Karl Marx, Selected Writings in Sociology and Social Philosophy*.

with the concept of transforming reality, since the transformation of an imaginary reality is an absurdity. Thus in both conceptions of consciousness there can be no true praxis. Praxis is only possible where the objective–subjective dialectic is maintained.[7]

Behaviourism also fails to comprehend the dialectic of men–world relationships. Under the form called mechanistic behaviourism, men are negated because they are seen as machines. The second form, logical behaviourism, also negates men, since it affirms that men's consciousness is 'merely an abstraction'.[8] The process of 'conscientization' cannot be founded upon any of these defective explanations of man–world relationships. 'Conscientization' is viable only because men's consciousness, although conditioned, can recognize that it is conditioned. This 'critical' dimension of consciousness accounts for the goals men assign to their transforming acts upon the world. Because they are able to have goals, men alone are capable of envisaging the result of their action even before initiating the proposed action. They are beings who pro-ject, as Marx makes clear in *Capital*:

We presuppose labour in a form that stamps it as exclusively human. A spider conducts operations that resemble those of a weaver, and a bee puts to shame many an architect in the construction of her cells. But what distinguishes the worst architect from the best of the bees is this, that the architect raises his structure in imagination before he erects it in reality.

Although bees, as expert 'specialists', can identify the flower they need for making their honey, they do not vary their

7. In a discussion of man–world relationships during a 'culture circle' a Chilean peasant affirmed, 'I now see that there is no world without men.' When the educator asked, 'Suppose all men died, but there were still trees, animals, birds, rivers, and stars, wouldn't this be the world?' 'No,' replied the peasant, 'there would be no one to say, this is the world.'

8. We refer to behaviourism as studied in John Beloff's *The Existence of Mind*.

specialization. They cannot produce by-products. Their action upon the world is not accompanied by objectification; it lacks the critical reflection which characterizes men's tasks. Whereas animals adapt themselves to the world to survive, men modify the world in order *to be more*. In adapting themselves for the sake of survival, without ends to achieve and choices to make, animals cannot 'animalize' the world. 'Animalization' of the world would be intimately linked to the 'animalization' of animals, and this would presuppose in animals an awareness that they are incomplete, which would engage them in a permanent quest. In fact, however, while they skilfully construct their hives and 'manufacture' honey, bees remain bees in their contact with the world; they do not become more or less bees.[9]

For men, as beings of praxis, to transform the world is to humanize it, even if making the world human may not yet signify the humanization of men. It may simply mean impregnating the world with man's curious and inventive presence, imprinting it with the trace of his works. The process of transforming the world, which reveals this presence of man, can lead to his humanization as well as his dehumanization, to his growth or diminution. These alternatives reveal to man his problematic nature and pose a problem for him, requiring that he choose one path or the other. Often this very process of transformation ensnares man and his freedom to choose. Nevertheless, because they impregnate the world with their reflective presence, only men can humanize or dehumanize. Humanization is their utopia, which they announce in denouncing dehumanizing processes.

The reflectiveness and finality of men's relationships with the world would not be possible if these relationships did not occur in a historical as well as physical context. Without critical reflection there is no finality, nor does finality have meaning outside an uninterrupted temporal series of events. For men

9. 'The tiger does not "de-tigerize" itself,' said Ortega y Gasset in one of his works.

there is no *here* relative to a *there* which is not connected to a *now*, a *before*, and an *after*. Thus men's relationships with the world are *per se* historical, as are men themselves. Not only do men make the history which makes them, but they can recount the history of this mutual making. In becoming 'hominized', as Teilhard de Chardin puts it, in the process of evolution, men become capable of having a biography. Animals, on the contrary, are immersed in a time which belongs not to them, but to men.

There is a further fundamental distinction between man's relationships with the world and the animal's contacts with it: only men work. A horse, for example, lacks what is proper to man, what Marx refers to in his example of the bees: 'At the end of every labour-process, we get a result that already existed in the imagination of the labourer at its commencement.' (See *Capital*.) Action without this dimension is not work. In the fields as well as in the circus, the apparent work of horses reflects the work of men. Action is work not because of the greater or lesser physical effort expended in it by the acting organism, but because of the consciousness the subject has of his own effort, the possibility of programming action, of creating tools and using them to mediate between himself and the object of his action, of having purposes, of anticipating results. Still more, for action to be work, it must result in significant products, which while distinct from the active agent, at the same time condition him and become the object of his reflection.[10] As men act upon the world effectively, transforming it by their work, their consciousness is in turn historically and culturally

10. This is proper to men's social relations, which imply their relationship to their world. That is why the traditional aristocratic dichotomy be-between manual work and intellectual work is no more than a myth. All work engages the whole man as an indivisible unity. A factory hand's work can no more be divided into manual or intellectual than ours in writing this essay. The only distinction that can be made between these forms of work is the predominance of the kind of effort demanded by the work: muscular-nervous effort or intellectual effort. Concerning this point, see Antonio Gramsci's, *Cultura y Literatura*.

conditioned through the 'inversion of praxis'. According to the quality of this conditioning, men's consciousness attains various levels in the context of cultural-historical reality. We propose to analyse these levels of consciousness as a further step towards understanding the process of 'conscientization'.

Historical conditioning and levels of consciousness

To understand the levels of consciousness, we must understand cultural–historical reality as a superstructure in relation to an infrastructure. Therefore, we will try to discern, in relative rather than absolute terms, the fundamental characteristics of the historical–cultural configuration to which such levels correspond.

Our intention is not to attempt a study of the origins and historical evolution of consciousness, but to make a concrete introductory analysis of the levels of consciousness in Latin American reality. This does not invalidate such an analysis for other areas of the Third World, nor for those areas in the metropolises which identify themselves with the Third World as 'areas of silence'.

We will first study the historical–cultural configuration which we have called the 'culture of silence'. This mode of culture is a superstructural expression which conditions a special form of consciousness. The culture of silence 'overdetermines' the infrastructure in which it originates, as Althusser shows.

Understanding the culture of silence is possible only if it is taken as a totality which is itself part of a greater whole. In this greater whole we must also recognize the culture or cultures which determine the voice of the 'culture of silence'. We do not mean that the 'culture of silence' is an entity created by the metropolis in specialized laboratories and transported to the Third World. Neither is it true, however, that it emerges by spontaneous generation. The fact is that the 'culture of silence' is born in the relationship between the Third World and the metropolis. 'It is not the dominator who constructs a culture and imposes it on the dominated. This culture is the result of the structural relations between the dominated and the dominators.'[11] Thus, understanding the 'culture of silence' presupposes an analysis of dependence as a relational phenomenon which gives rise to different forms of being, of thinking, of expression, those of the 'culture of silence' and those of the culture which 'has a voice'.

We must avoid both of the positions previously criticized in this essay: objectivism, which leads to mechanism; and idealism, which leads to solipsism. Further, we must guard against idealizing the superstructure, dichotomizing it from the infrastructure. If we underestimate either the superstructure or infrastructure it will be impossible to explain the social structure itself. Social structure is not an abstraction; it exists in the dialectic between super- and infrastructures. Failing to understand this dialectic, we will not understand the dialectic of change and permanence as the expression of the social structure.

It is true that infrastructure, created in the relations by which the work of man transforms the world, gives rise to superstructure. But it is also true that the latter, mediated by men, who introject its myths, turns upon the infrastructure and 'overdetermines' it. If it were not for the dynamic of these precarious relationships in which men exist and work in the world, we could speak neither of social structure, nor of men, nor of a human world.

Let us return to the relationship between the metropolitan society and the dependent society as the source of their respective ways of being, thinking and expression. Both the metropolitan society and the dependent society, totalities in themselves, are part of a greater whole, the economic, historical, cultural, and political context in which their mutual relationships evolve. Though the context in which these societies relate

11. José Luis Fiori, in a letter to the author. José Luis Fiori was an assistant to the author on his Chilean team in ICIRA, one of the best institutes of its type in the Third World.

to each other is the same, the quality of the relationship is obviously different in each case, being determined by the role which each plays in the total context of their interrelation. The action of the metropolitan society upon the dependent society has a directive character, whereas the object society's action, whether it be response or initiative, has a dependent character.

The relationships between the dominator and the dominated reflect the greater social context, even when formally personal. Such relationships imply the introjection by the dominated of the cultural myths of the dominator. Similarly, the dependent society introjects the values and life style of the metropolitan society, since the structure of the latter shapes that of the former. This results in the duality of the dependent society, its ambiguity, its being and not being itself, and the ambivalence characteristic of its long experience of dependency, both attracted by and rejecting the metropolitan society.

The infrastructure of the dependent society is shaped by the director society's will. The resultant superstructure, therefore, reflects the inauthenticity of the infrastructure. Whereas the metropolis can absorb its ideological crises through mechanisms of economic power and a highly developed technology, the dependent structure is too weak to support the slightest popular manifestation. This accounts for the frequent rigidity of the dependent structure.

The dependent society is by definition a silent society. Its voice is not an authentic voice, but merely an echo of the voice of the metropolis – in every way, the metropolis speaks, the dependent society listens.[12]

The silence of the object society in relation to the director

12. It is interesting to note how this happens with the churches. The concept of 'mission lands' originates in the metropolis. For a mission land to exist, there must be another which defines it as such. There is a significant coincidence between mission-sending nations and metropolises as there is between mission lands and the Third World. It would seem to us that, on the contrary, all lands constitute mission territory to the Christian perspective.

society is repeated in the relationships within the object society itself. Its power elites, silent in the face of the metropolis, silence their own people in turn. Only when the people of a dependent society break out of the culture of silence and win their right to speak – only, that is, when radical structural changes transform the dependent society – can such a society as a whole cease to be silent towards the director society.

On the other hand, if a group seizes power through a *coup d'état*, as in the recent case of Peru, and begins to take nationalist economic and cultural defence measures, its policy creates a new contradiction, with one of the following consequences. Firstly, the new regime may exceed its own intentions and be obliged to break definitively with the 'culture of silence' both internally and externally. Or, fearing the ascendancy of the people, it may retrogress, and re-impose silence on the people. Thirdly, the government may sponsor a new type of populism. Stimulated by the first nationalist measures, the submerged masses would have the illusion that they were participating in the trans-formations of their society, when, in fact, they were being shrewdly manipulated. In Peru, as the military group which took power in 1968 pursues its political objectives, many of its actions will cause 'cracks' to appear in the most closed areas of Peruvian society. Through these cracks, the masses will begin to emerge from their silence with increasingly demanding attitudes. Insofar as their demands are met, the masses will tend not only to increase their frequency, but also to alter their nature.

Thus, the populist approach will also end up creating serious contradictions for the power group. It will find itself obliged either to break open the culture of silence or to restore it. That is why it seems to us difficult in Latin America's present histori-cal moment for any government to maintain even a relatively aggressive independent policy towards the metropolis while preserving the culture of silence internally.

In 1961, Janio Quadros came to power in Brazil in what was perhaps the greatest electoral victory in the nation's history. He attempted to carry out a paradoxical policy of independence towards the metropolis and control over the people. After seven months in office, he unexpectedly announced to the nation that he was obliged to renounce the presidency under pressure from the same hidden forces which had driven President Getulio Vargas to commit suicide. And so he made a melancholy exit and headed for London.

The Brazilian military group which overthrew the Goulart government in 1964, picturesquely designating their action a revolution, have followed a coherent course according to our preceding analysis: a consistent policy of servility towards the metropolis and the violent imposition of silence upon their own people. A policy of servility towards the metropolis and rupture of the internal culture of silence would not be viable. Neither would a policy of independence towards the metropolis while maintaining the culture of silence internally.

Latin American societies were established as closed societies from the time of their conquest by the Spanish and Portuguese, when the culture of silence took shape. With the exception of post-revolutionary Cuba, these societies are still closed societies today.[13] They are dependent societies for whom only the poles of decision of which they are the object have changed at different historical moments: Portugal, Spain, England or the United States.

Latin American societies are closed societies characterized by a rigid hierarchical social structure; by the lack of internal markets, since their economy is controlled from the outside; by the exportation of raw materials and importation of manufactured goods, without a voice in either process; by a precarious and selective educational system whose schools are an instrument of maintaining the *status quo*; by high percentages of illiteracy and disease, including the naïvely named 'tropical diseases' which are really diseases of underdevelopment and

13. *Re* 'closed societies', see, Henri Bergson's *The Two Sources of Morality and Religion*, and Karl Popper's *The Open Society and Its Enemies*.

dependence; by alarming rates of infant mortality; by malnutrition, often with irreparable effects on mental faculties; by a low life expectancy; and by a high rate of crime.

There is a mode of consciousness which corresponds to the concrete reality of such dependent societies. It is a consciousness historically conditioned by the social structures. The principal characteristic of this consciousness, as dependent as the society to whose structure it conforms, is its 'quasi-adherence' to objective reality, or 'quasi-immersion' in reality.[14] As I make clear in *Pedagogy of the Oppressed*, the dominated consciousness does not have sufficient distance from reality to objectify it in order to know it in a critical way. We call this mode of consciousness 'semi-intransitive' (see my *Educação como Prática da Liberdade*).

Semi-intransitive consciousness is typical of closed structures. In its quasi-immersion in concrete reality, this consciousness fails to perceive many of reality's challenges, or perceives them in a distorted way. Its semi-intransitiveness is a kind of obliteration imposed by objective conditions. Because of this obliteration, the only data which the dominated consciousness grasps are the data which lie within the orbit of its lived experience. This mode of consciousness cannot objectify the facts and problematical situations of daily life. Men whose consciousness exists at this level of quasi-immersion lack what we call 'structural perception', which shapes and reshapes itself from concrete reality in the apprehension of facts and problematical situations. Lacking structural perception, men attribute the sources of such facts and situations in their lives either to some superreality or to something within themselves; in either case to something outside objective reality. It is not hard to trace here the origin of the fatalistic attitudes men adopt in certain

14. This mode of consciousness is still found to be predominant in Latin American rural areas where large property holdings (*latifundios*) are the rule. The rural areas constitute 'closed societies' which maintain the 'culture of silence' intact.

situations. If the explanation for those situations lies in a superior power, or in men's own 'natural' incapacity, it is obvious that their action will not be orientated towards transforming reality, but towards those superior beings responsible for the problematical situation, or towards that presumed incapacity. Their action, therefore, has the character of defensive magic or therapeutic magic. Thus, before harvest time or sowing, Latin American peasants, and the peasants of the Third World in general, perform magical rites, often of a syncretistic religious nature. Even when those rites evolve into cultural traditions, they remain instrumental for a time; the transformation of a magical rite into an expression of tradition does not happen suddenly. It is a process involving, once again, the dialectic between objectivity and subjectivity.[15]

Under the impact of infrastructural changes which produced the first 'cracks' in Latin American societies, they entered the present stage of historical and cultural transition – some more intensely than others. In the particular case of Brazil, this process began with the abolition of slavery at the end of the nineteenth century.[16] It accelerated during the First World War and again after the depression of 1929, intensified during the Second World War, and continued with fits and starts to 1964, when the military coup violently returned the nation to silence.

15. It is essential that modernization of backward structures eject the sources of the magic rites which are an integral part of the structures. If not, while it may do away with the phenomenon of magic rites themselves, modernization will proceed to mythologize technology. The myth of technology will replace the magical entities which formerly explained problematical situations. Further, the myth of technology might be seen, not as the substitute for the old forces which, in this case, continue to exist, but as something superior even to them. Technology would thus be projected as all-powerful, beyond all structures, accessible only to a few privileged men.

16. The abolition of slavery in Brazil brought about the inversion of capital in incipient industries, and stimulated the first waves of German, Italian and Japanese immigration to the southern central and southern Brazilian states.

What is important, nevertheless, is that once the cracks in the structure begin to appear, and once societies enter the period of transition, immediately the first movements of emergence of the hitherto submerged and silent masses begin to manifest themselves. This does not mean, however, that movements towards emergence automatically break open the culture of silence. In their relationship to the metropolis, transitional societies continue to be silent totalities. Within them, however, the phenomenon of the emerging masses forces the power elites to experiment with new forms of maintaining the masses in silence, since structural changes which provoke the emergence of the masses also qualitatively alter their quasi-immersed and semi-intransitive consciousness.

The objective datum of a closed society, one of its structural components, is the silence of the masses, a silence broken only by occasional, ineffective rebellions. When this silence coincides with the masses' fatalistic perception of reality, the power elites which impose silence on the masses are rarely questioned.[17] When the closed society begins to crack, however, the new datum becomes the demanding presence of the masses. Silence is no longer seen as an unalterable given, but as the result of a reality which can and must be transformed. This historical transition, lived by Latin American societies to a greater or lesser degree, corresponds to a new phase of popular consciousness, that of 'naïve transitivity'. Formerly the popular consciousness was semi-intransitive, limited to meeting the challenges relative to biological needs. In the process of emerg-

17. Although we have not made a precise study of the emergence of black consciousness in the United States, we are tempted to state that, especially in southern areas, there are divergences between the younger and older generations which cannot be explained by psychological criteria, but rather by a dialectical understanding of the process of the emerging consciousness. The younger generation, less influenced by fatalism than the older, must logically assume positions qualitatively different from the older generation, not only in regard to passive silence, but also in regard to the methods used by their protest movements.

ing from silence, the capacity of the popular consciousness expands so that men begin to be able to visualize and distinguish what before was not clearly outlined.

Although the qualitative difference between the semi-intransitive consciousness and the naïve transitive consciousness can be explained by the phenomenon of emergence due to structural transformations in society, there are no rigidly defined frontiers between the historical moments which produce qualitative changes in men's awareness. In many respects, the semi-intransitive consciousness remains present in the naïve transitive consciousness. In Latin America, for example, almost the entire peasant population is still in the stage of quasi-immersion, a stage with a much longer history than the present one of emergence. The semi-intransitive peasant consciousness introjected innumerable myths in the former stage which continue despite a change in awareness towards transitivity. Therefore, the transitive consciousness emerges as a naïve consciousness, as dominated as the former. Nevertheless, it is now indisputably more disposed to perceiving the source of its ambiguous existence in the objective conditions of society.

The emergence of the popular consciousness implies, if not the overcoming of the culture of silence, at least the presence of the masses in the historical process applying pressure on the power elite. It can only be understood as one dimension of a more complex phenomenon. That is to say, the emergence of the popular consciousness, although yet naïvely intransitive, is also a moment in the developing consciousness of the power elite. In a structure of domination, the silence of the popular masses would not exist but for the power elites who silence them; nor would there be a power elite without the masses. Just as there is a moment of surprise among the masses when they begin to see what they did not see before, there is a corresponding surprise among the elites in power when they find themselves unmasked by the masses. This two-fold unveiling provokes anxieties in both the masses and the power elites. The masses become anxious for freedom, anxious to overcome the silence in which they have always existed. The elites are anxious to maintain the *status quo* by allowing only superficial transformations designed to prevent any real change in their power of prescription.

In the transitional process, the predominantly static character of the 'closed society' gradually yields to a dynamism in all dimensions of social life. Contradictions come to the surface, provoking conflicts in which the popular consciousness becomes more and more demanding, causing greater and greater alarm on the part of the elites. As the lines of this historical transition become more sharply etched, illuminating the contradictions inherent in a dependent society, groups of intellectuals and students, who themselves belong to the privileged elite, seek to become engaged in social reality, tending to reject imported schemes and prefabricated solutions. The arts gradually cease to be the mere expression of the easy life of the affluent bourgeoisie, and begin to find their inspiration in the hard life of the people. Poets begin to write about more than their lost loves, and even the theme of lost love becomes less maudlin, more objective and lyrical. They speak now of the field hand and worker not as abstract and metaphysical concepts, but as concrete men with concrete lives.[18]

In the case of Brazil, such qualitative changes marked all levels of creative life. As the transitional phase intensified, these active groups focused more and more on their national reality in order to know it better and to create ways of overcoming their society's state of dependency.

The transitional phase also generates a new style of political life, since the old political models of the closed society are no longer adequate where the masses are an emerging historical presence. In the closed society, relations between the elite and

18. See the excellent study on 'The role of poetry in the Mozambican revolution' in *Africa Today*.

the quasi-immersed people are mediated by political bosses, representing the various elitist factions. In Brazil, the invariably paternalistic political bosses are owners not only of their lands, but also of the silent and obedient popular masses under their control. As rural areas in Latin America at first were not touched by the emergence provoked by the cracks in society, they remained predominantly under the control of the political bosses.[19] In urban centres, by contrast, a new kind of leadership emerged to mediate between the power elites and the emerging masses: the populist leadership. There is one characteristic of populist leadership which deserves our particular attention: we refer to its manipulative character.

Although the emergence of the masses from silence does not allow the political style of the formerly closed society to continue, that does not mean that the masses are able to speak on their own behalf. They have merely passed from quasi-immersion to a naïve transitive state of awareness. Populist leadership thus could be said to be an adequate response to the new presence of the masses in the historical process. But it is a manipulative leadership – manipulative of the masses, since it cannot manipulate the elite.

Populist manipulation of the masses must be seen from two different perspectives. On the one hand, it is undeniably a kind of political opiate which maintains not only the naïveté of the emerging consciousness, but also the people's habit of being directed. On the other hand, to the extent that it uses mass protest and demands, political manipulation paradoxically accelerates the process by which the people unveil reality. This paradox sums up the ambiguous character of populism; it is

19. In Latin America, the Mexican, Bolivian and Cuban revolutions broke open the closed structures of rural areas. Only Cuba, however, succeeded in making this change permanent. Mexico frustrated its revolution, and the Bolivian revolutionary movement was defeated. Nevertheless, the presence of the peasant in the social life of both Mexico and Bolivia is an indisputable fact as a result of that initial opening.

manipulative, yet at the same time a factor in democratic mobilization.[20]

Thus, the new style of political life found in transitional societies is not confined to the manipulative role of its leaders, mediating between the masses and the elites. Indeed, the populist style of political action ends up creating conditions for youth groups and intellectuals to exercise political participation together with the people. Although it is an instance of manipulative paternalism, populism offers the possibility of a critical analysis of the manipulation itself. Within the whole play of contradictions and ambiguities, the emergence of the popular masses in transitional societies prepares the way for the masses to become conscious of their dependent state.

As we have said, the passage of the masses from a semi-intransitive to a naïve transitive state of consciousness is also the moment of an awakening consciousness on the part of the elites, a decisive moment for the critical consciousness of progressive groups. At first there appears a fragile awareness among small groups of intellectuals who are still marked by the cultural alienation of society as a whole, an alienation reinforced by their university 'formation'. As the contradictions typical of a society in transition emerge more clearly, these groups multiply and are able to distinguish more and more precisely what makes up their society. They tend more and more to join with the popular masses in a variety of ways: through literature, plastic arts, the theatre, music, education, sports and folk art. What is important is the communion with the people which some of these groups are able to achieve.

At this point the increasingly critical consciousness of these progressive groups, arising from the naïve transitivity of the

20. Francisco Weffort, in his introduction to my *Educação como Prática da Liberdade*, points out that ambiguity is the principal characteristic of populism. A professor of sociology, Mr Weffort is one of the best Brazilian analysts of populism today. The Center for the Study of Development and Social Change, Cambridge, Massachusetts, has recently issued a translation of this introduction, by Loretta Slover, for restricted circulation.

emerging masses, becomes a challenge to the consciousness of the power elites. Societies which find themselves in this historical phase, which cannot be clearly understood outside the critical comprehension of the totality of which they are a part, live in a climate of pre-revolution whose dialectical contradiction is the *coup d'état*.

In Latin America, the *coup d'état* has become the answer of the economic and military power elites to the crises of popular emergence. This response varies with the relative influence of the military. According to the degree of its violence and that of the subsequent repression of the people, the *coup d'état* 'reactivates' old patterns of behaviour in the people, patterns which belong to their former state of quasi-immersion. Only this 'reactivation' of the 'culture of silence' can explain the passivity of the people when faced with the violence and arbitrary rule of Latin American military coups (with the sole exception, up to now, of Peru).[21]

It must be emphasized that the *coups d'état* in Latin America are incomprehensible without a dialectical vision of reality; any attempt to understand them mechanistically will lead to a distorted picture. Intensely problematical, unmasking more and more their condition of dependency, Latin American societies in transition are confronted with two contradictory possibilities: revolution or *coup d'état*. The stronger the ideological foundations of a *coup d'état*, the more it is impossible for a society to return afterwards to the same political style which created the very conditions for the coup. A *coup d'état* qualitatively alters the process of a society's historical transition, and marks the beginning of a new transition. In the original transitional stage, the coup was the antithetical alternative to revolution; in the new transitional stage, the coup is defined and confirmed as an arbitrary and anti-popular power, whose tendency before the

21. By the same phenomenon of the people's reversion to silence, Althusser explains how it was possible for the Russian people to put up with the crimes of Stalin's repression.

continuing possibility of revolution is to become more and more rigid.

In Brazil, the transition marked by the *coup d'état* sets up recapitulation to an ideology of development based on the handing over of the national economy to foreign interests, an ideology in which 'the idea of the great international enterprise replaces the idea of the state monopoly as the basis for development', to quote Cardoso. One of the basic requirements for such an ideology is necessarily the silencing of popular sectors and their consequent removal from the sphere of decision-making. Popular forces must, therefore, avoid the naïve illusion that this transitional stage may afford 'openings' which will enable them to re-establish the rhythm of the previous transitional stage, whose political model corresponded to a national populist ideology of development.

The 'openings' which the new transitional phase offers have their own semantics. Such openings do not signify a return to what has been, but a give and take within the play of accommodations demanded by the reigning ideology. Whatever its ideology, the new transitional phase challenges the popular forces to find an entirely new way of proceeding, distinct from their action in the former period when they were contending with the forces which those coups brought to power.

One of the reasons for the change is obvious enough. Due to the repression imposed by the coup, the popular forces have to act in silence, and silent action requires a difficult apprenticeship. Further, the popular forces have to search for ways to counter the effects of the reactivation of the culture of silence, which historically engendered the dominated consciousness.

Under these conditions, what is the possibility of survival for the emerging consciousness which has reached the state of naïve transitivity? The answer to this question must be found in a deeper analysis of the transitional phase inaugurated by the military coup. Since revolution is still a possibility in this phase, our analysis will focus on the dialectical confrontation between the revolutionary project (or, lamentably, projects) and the new regime.

Cultural action and cultural revolution

It would be unnecessary to tell the revolutionary groups that they are the antagonistic contradiction of the Right. However, it would not be inexpedient to emphasize that this antagonism, which is born of their opposing purposes, must express itself in a behaviour which is equally antagonistic. There ought to be a difference in the praxis of the Right and of revolutionary groups which defines them to the people, making the options of each group explicit. This difference between the two groups stems from the utopic nature of the revolutionary groups, and the impossibility of the Right to be utopic. This is not an arbitrary distinction, but one which is sufficient to distinguish radically the objectives and forms of action taken by the revolutionary and Rightist groups.[22]

To the extent that real utopia implies the denunciation of an unjust reality and the proclamation of a pre-project, revolutionary leadership cannot:

1. Denounce reality without knowing reality.

2. Proclaim a new reality without having a draft project which, although it emerges in the denunciation, becomes a viable project only in praxis.

3. Know reality without relying on the people as well as on objective facts for the source of its knowledge.

4. Denounce and proclaim by itself.

5. Make new myths out of the denunciation and annunciation – denunciation and annunciation must be anti-ideological in so far as they result from a scientific knowledge of reality.

6. Renounce communion with the people, not only during the

22. Re radicalization and its opposite, sectarianism, see my *Pedagogy of the Oppressed*.

time between the dialectic of denunciation and annunciation and the concretization of a viable project, but also in the very act of giving that project concrete reality.

Thus, revolutionary leadership falls into internal contradictions which compromise its purpose, when, victim of a fatalist concept of history, it tries to domesticate the people mechanically to a future which the leadership knows *a priori*, but which it thinks the people are incapable of knowing. In this case, revolutionary leadership ceases to be utopian and ends up identified with the Right. The Right makes no denunciation or proclamation, except, as we have said, to denounce whoever denounces it and to proclaim its own myths.

A true revolutionary project, on the other hand, to which the utopian dimension is natural, is a process in which the people assume the role of subject in the precarious adventure of transforming and recreating the world. The Right is necessarily opposed to such a project, and attempts to immobilize it. Thus, to use Erich Fromm's terms, the revolutionary utopia is biophilic, whereas the Right in its rigidity is necrophilic, as is a revolutionary leadership which has become bureaucratic.[23]

Revolutionary utopia tends to be dynamic rather than static; tends to life rather than death; to the future as a challenge to man's creativity rather than as a repetition of the present; to love as liberation of subjects rather than as pathological possessiveness; to the emotion of life rather than cold abstractions; to living together in harmony rather than gregariousness: to dialogue rather than muteness; to praxis rather than 'law and order'; to men who organize themselves reflectively for action rather than men who are organized for passivity; to creative and communicative language rather than prescriptive signals; to reflective challenges rather than domesticating slogans; and to values which are lived rather than myths which are imposed.

The Right in its rigidity prefers the dead to the living; the

23. Re biophilia and necrophilia, see Erich Fromm's *The Heart of Man*.

static to the dynamic; the future as a repetition of the past rather than as a creative venture; pathological forms of love rather than real love; frigid schematization rather than the emotion of living; gregariousness rather than authentic living together; organization men rather than men who organize; imposed myths rather than incarnated values; directives rather than creative and communicative language; and slogans rather than challenges.

It is necessary for revolutionaries to witness more and more to the radical difference which separates them from the Rightist elite. It is not enough to condemn the violence of the Right, its aristocratic posture, its myths. Revolutionaries must prove their respect for the people, their belief and confidence in them, not as a mere strategy but as an implicit requirement to being a revolutionary. This commitment to the people is fundamental at any given moment, but especially in the transition period created by a *coup d'état*.

Victimizing the people by its violence, the coup re-imposes, as we have said, the old climate of the 'culture of silence'. The people, standing at the threshhold of their experience as subjects and participants of society, need signs that will help them recognize who is with them and who is against them. These signs, or witnesses, are given through projects proposed by men in dialectic with the structure. Each project constitutes an interacting totality of objectives, methods, procedures and techniques. The revolutionary project is distinguished from the Rightist project not only by its objectives, but by its total reality. A project's method cannot be dichotomized from its content and objectives, as if methods were neutral and equally appropriate for liberation or domination. Such a concept reveals a naïve idealism which is satisfied with the subjective intention of the person who acts.

The revolutionary project is engaged in a struggle against oppressive and dehumanizing structures. To the extent that it seeks the affirmation of concrete men as men freeing themselves, any thoughtless concession to the oppressor's methods is always a danger and a threat to the revolutionary project itself. Revolutionaries must demand of themselves an imperious coherence. As men, they may make mistakes, they are subject to equivocation, but they cannot act like reactionaries and call themselves revolutionaries. They must suit their action to historical conditions, taking advantage of the real and unique possibilities which exist. Their role is to seek the most efficient and viable means of helping the people to move from the levels of semi-intransitive or naïve-transitive consciousness to the level of critical consciousness. This preoccupation, which is alone authentically liberating, is implicit in the revolutionary project itself. Originating in the praxis of both the leadership and the rank and file, every revolutionary project is basically 'cultural action' in the process of becoming 'cultural revolution'.

Revolution is a critical process, unrealizable without science and reflection. In the midst of reflective action on the world to be transformed, the people come to recognize that the world is indeed being transformed. The world in transformation is the mediator of the dialogue between the people, at one pole of the act of knowing, and the revolutionary leadership, at the other. If objective conditions do not always permit this dialogue its existence can be verified by the witness of the leadership.

Che Guevara is an example of the unceasing witness revolutionary leadership gives to dialogue with the people. The more we study his work, the more we perceive his conviction that anyone who wants to become a true revolutionary must be in 'communion' with the people. Guevara did not hesitate to recognize the capacity to love as an indispensable condition for authentic revolutionaries. While he constantly noted the failure of the peasants to participate in the guerrilla movement, his references to them in the *Bolivian Diary* did not express disaffection. He never lost hope of ultimately being able to count on their participation. In the same spirit of communion, Guevara's guerrilla encampment served as the 'theoretical context' in which he and his companions together analysed the concrete events they were living through and planned the strategy of their action.

Guevara did not create dichotomies between the methods, content and objectives of his projects. In spite of the risks to his and his companions' lives, he justified guerrilla warfare as an introduction to freedom, as a call to life to those who are the living dead. Like Camilo Torres, he became a guerrilla not out of desperation, but because, as a lover of men, he dreamt of a new man being born in the experience of liberation. In this sense, Guevara incarnated the authentic revolutionary utopia as did few others. He was one of the great prophets of the silent ones of the Third World. Conversant with many of them, he spoke on behalf of all of them.

In citing Guevara and his witness as a guerrilla, we do not mean to say that revolutionaries elsewhere are obliged to repeat the same witness. What is essential is that they strive to achieve communion with the people as he did, patiently and unceasingly. Communion with the people – accessible only to those with a utopian vision, in the sense referred to in this essay – is one of the fundamental characteristics of cultural action for freedom. Authentic communion implies communication between men, mediated by the world. Only praxis in the context of communion makes 'conscientization' a viable project. 'Conscientization' is a joint project in that it takes place in a man among other men, men united by their action and by their reflection upon that action and upon the world. Thus men together achieve the state of perceptive clarity which Goldmann calls 'the maximum of potential consciousness' beyond 'real consciousness'.

'Conscientization' is more than a simple *prise de conscience*. While it implies overcoming 'false consciousness', overcoming, that is, a semi-intransitive or naïve transitive state of consciousness, it implies further the critical insertion of the conscientized person into a demythologized reality. This is why 'conscientization' is an unrealizable project for the Right. The Right is by its nature incapable of being utopian, and hence it cannot develop a form of cultural action which would bring about 'conscientization'. There can be no 'conscientization' of the people without a radical denunciation of dehumanizing structures, accompanied by the proclamation of a new reality to be created by men. The Right cannot unmask itself, nor can it sponsor the means for the people to unmask it more than it is willing to be unmasked. With the increased clarity of the popular consciousness, its own consciousness tends to grow, but this form of 'conscientization' cannot convert itself into a praxis leaning to the 'conscientization' of the people. There can be no 'conscientization' without denunciation of unjust structures, a thing which cannot be expected of the Right. Nor can there be popular 'conscientization' for domination. The Right invents new forms of cultural action only for domination.

Thus, the two forms of cultural action are antagonistic to each other. Whereas cultural action for freedom is characterized by dialogue, and its pre-eminent purpose is to conscientize the people, cultural action for domination is opposed to dialogue and serves to domesticate the people. The former problematizes, the latter sloganizes.[24] Since cultural action for freedom is committed to the scientific unveiling of reality, to the exposure, that is, of myths and ideologies, it must separate ideology from science. Althusser, in *Para Leer el Capital*, insists on the necessity of this separation. Cultural action for freedom can be satisfied neither with 'the mystifications of ideology', as he calls them, nor with 'a simple moral denunciation of myths and errors', but must undertake a 'rational and rigorous critique [of ideology]'. The fundamental role of those committed to cultural action for conscientization is not properly speaking to fabricate the liberating idea, but to invite the people to grasp with their minds the truth of their reality.

Consistent with this spirit of knowing, scientific knowledge

24. In *Pedagogy of the Oppressed*, I discuss both these forms of cultural action.

cannot be knowledge that is merely transmitted, for it would itself become ideological myth, even if it were transmitted with the intention of liberating men. The discrepancy between intention and practice would be resolved in favour of practice. The only authentic points of departure for the scientific knowledge of reality are the dialectical relationships between men and the world, and the critical comprehension of how these relationships are evolved and how they in turn condition men's perception of concrete reality.

Those who use cultural action as a strategy for maintaining their domination over the people have no choice but to indoctrinate the people in a mythified version of reality. In doing so, the Right subordinates science and technology to its own ideology, using them to disseminate information and prescriptions in its effort to adjust the people to the reality which the 'communications' media define as proper. By contrast, for those who undertake cultural action for freedom, science is the indispensable instrument for denouncing the myths created by the Right, and philosophy is the matrix of the proclamation of a new reality. Science and philosophy together provide the principles of action for 'conscientization'. Cultural action for 'conscientization' is always a utopian enterprise. That is why it needs philosophy, without which, instead of denouncing reality and announcing the future, it would fall into the 'mystification of ideological knowledge'.

The utopian nature of cultural action for freedom is what distinguishes it above all from cultural action for domination. Cultural action for domination, based on myths, cannot pose problems about reality to the people, nor orientate the people to the unveiling of reality, since both of these projects would imply denunciation and annunciation. On the contrary, in the problematizing and conscientizing of cultural action for freedom, the annunciation of a new reality is the historical project proposed for men's achievement.

In the face of a semi-intransitive or naïve state of consciousness among the people, 'conscientization' envisages their attaining critical consciousness, or 'the maximum of potential consciousness'. This objective cannot terminate when the annunciation becomes concrete. On the contrary, when the annunciation becomes concrete reality, the need becomes even greater for critical consciousness among the people, both horizontally and vertically. Thus, cultural action for freedom, which characterized the movement which struggled for the realization of what was announced, must then transform itself into permanent cultural revolution.

Before going on to elaborate upon the distinct but essentially related moments of cultural action and cultural revolution, let us summarize our preceding points about levels of consciousness. An explicit relationship has been established between cultural action for freedom, conscientization as its chief enterprise, and the transcendence of semi-intransitive and naïve-transitive states of consciousness by critical consciousness. Critical consciousness is brought about not through an intellectual effort alone, but through praxis – through the authentic union of action and reflection. Such reflective action cannot be denied to the people. If it were, the people would be no more than activist pawns in the hands of a leadership which reserved for itself the right of decision-making. The authentic Left cannot fail to stimulate the overcoming of the people's false consciousness, on whatever level it exists, just as the Right is incapable of doing so. In order to maintain its power, the Right needs an elite who think for it, assisting it in accomplishing its projects. Revolutionary leadership needs the people in order to make the revolutionary project a reality, but the people in the process of becoming more and more critically conscious.

After the revolutionary reality is inaugurated, 'conscientization' continues to be indispensable. It is the instrument for ejecting the cultural myths which the people retain despite the new reality. Further, it is a force countering the bureaucracy, which threatens to deaden the revolutionary vision and domi-

nate the people in the very name of their freedom.[25] Finally,
'conscientization' is a defence against another threat, that of the
potential mythification of the technology which the new society
requires to transform its backward infrastructures (see my
Pedagogy of the Oppressed).

There are two possible directions open to the transitive
popular consciousness. The first is growth from a naïve state of
consciousness to the level of critical consciousness – Goldmann's 'maximum of potential consciousness'. The second is
the distortion of the transitive state of consciousness to its pathological form – that of the fanatic or 'irrational' consciousness –
as Gabriel Marcel described in *Man Against Mass Society*.
This form has a mythical character which replaces the magical
character of the semi-intransitive and naïve-transitive states of
consciousness. 'Massification' – the phenomenon of mass
societies – originates at this level. Mass society is not to be
associated with the emergence of the masses in the historical
process, as an aristocratic eye may view the phenomenon.
True, the emergence of the masses with their claims and demands makes them present in the historical process, however
naïve their consciousness – a phenomenon which accompanies
the cracking up of closed societies under the impact of the first
infrastructural changes. Mass society, however, occurs much
later. It appears in highly technologized, complex societies. In
order to function, these societies require specialties, which
become 'specialisms', and rationality, which degenerates into
myth-making irrationalism.

Distinct from specialties, to which we are not opposed,
specialisms narrow the area of knowledge in such a way that
the so-called 'specialists' become generally incapable of thinking. Because they have lost the vision of the whole of which

25. One must reject the myth that any criticism of necrophilic bureau-
cracies which swallow up revolutionary proclamation strengthens the
Right. The opposite is true. Silence, not criticism, in this case would
renounce the proclamation and be a capitulation to the Right.

their 'specialty' is only one dimension, they cannot even think correctly in the area of their specialization.

Similarly, the rationality basic to science and technology disappears under the extraordinary effects of technology itself, and its place is taken by myth-making irrationalism. The attempt to explain man as a superior type of robot originates in such irrationalism.[26]

In mass society, ways of thinking become as standardized as ways of dressing and tastes in food. Men begin thinking and acting according to the prescriptions they receive daily from the communications media rather than in response to their dialectical relationships with the world. In mass societies, where everything is prefabricated and behaviour is almost automatized, men are lost because they don't have to 'risk themselves'. They do not have to think about even the smallest things; there is always some manual which says what to do in situation 'A' or 'B'. Rarely do men have to pause at a street corner to think which direction to follow. There's always an arrow which de-problematizes the situation. Though street signs are not evil in themselves, and are necessary in cosmopolitan cities, they are among thousands of directional signals in a technological society which, introjected by men, hinder their capacity for critical thinking.

Technology thus ceases to be perceived by men as one of the greatest expressions of their creative power and becomes instead a species of new divinity to which they create a cult of worship. Efficiency ceases to be identified with the power that men have to think, to imagine, to risk themselves in creation, and rather comes to mean carrying out orders from above precisely and punctually.[27]

26. In a recent conversation with me, the psychoanalyst Michael Maccoby, Dr Fromm's assistant, stated that his research suggests a relationship between mythologizing technology and necrophilic attitudes.

27. 'Professionals who seek self-realization through creative and autonomous behaviour without regard to the defined goals, needs and channels of their respective departments have no more place in a large corporation

Let it be clear, however, that technological development must be one of the concerns of the revolutionary project. It would be simplistic to attribute responsibility for these deviations to technology in itself. This would be another kind of irrationalism, that of conceiving of technology as a demonic entity, above and opposed to men. Critically viewed, technology is nothing more nor less than a natural phase of the creative process which engaged man from the moment he forged his first tool and began to transform the world for its humanization.

Considering that technology is not only necessary but part of man's natural development, the question facing revolutionaries is how to avoid technology's mythical deviations. The techniques of 'human relations' are not the answer, for in the final analysis they are only another way of domesticating and alienating men even further in the service of greater productivity. For this and other reasons which we have expounded in the course of this essay, we insist on cultural action for freedom. We do not, however, attribute to 'conscientization' any magical power, which would only be to mythify it. 'Conscientization' is not a magical charm for revolutionaries, but a basic dimension of their reflective action. If men were not 'conscious bodies', capable of acting and perceiving, of knowing and re-creating, if they were not conscious of themselves and the world, the idea of 'conscientization' would make no sense – but then, neither would the idea of revolution. Authentic revolutions are undertaken in order to liberate men, precisely because men can know themselves to be oppressed, and be conscious of the oppressive reality in which they exist.

But since, as we have seen, men's consciousness is conditioned by reality, 'conscientization' is first of all the effort to enlighten

---

or government agency than squeamish soldiers in the Army.... The social organization of the new Technology, by systematically denying to the general population experiences which are analogous to those of its higher management, contributes very heavily to the growth of social irrationality in our society', to quote John MacDermott.

men about the obstacles preventing them from a clear perception of reality. In this role, 'conscientization' effects the ejection of cultural myths which confuse the people's awareness and make them ambiguous beings.

Because men are historical beings, incomplete and conscious of being incomplete, revolution is as natural and permanent a human dimension as is education. Only a mechanistic mentality holds that education can cease at a certain point, or that revolution can be halted when it attains power. To be authentic, revolution must be a continuous event. Otherwise it will cease to be revolution, and will become sclerotic bureaucracy.

Revolution is always cultural, whether it be in the phase of denouncing an oppressive society and proclaiming the advent of a just society, or in the phase of the new society inaugurated by the revolution. In the new society, the revolutionary process becomes cultural revolution.

Finally, let us clarify the reasons why we have been speaking of cultural action and cultural revolution as distinct moments in the revolutionary process. In the first place, cultural action for freedom is carried out in opposition to the dominating power elite, while cultural revolution takes place in harmony with the revolutionary regime – although this does not mean that it is subordinated to the revolutionary power. All cultural revolution proposes freedom as its goal. Cultural action, on the contrary, if sponsored by the oppressive regime, can be a strategy for domination, in which case it can never become cultural revolution.

The limits of cultural action are set by the oppressive reality itself and by the silence imposed by the power elite. The nature of the oppression, therefore, determines the tactics, which are necessarily different from those employed in cultural revolution. Whereas cultural action for freedom confronts silence both as external fact and introjected reality, cultural revolution confronts it only as introjected reality. Both cultural action for freedom and cultural revolution are an effort to negate the dominating culture culturally, even before the new culture resulting from that negation has become reality. The new cultural reality itself is continuously subject to negation in favour of the increasing affirmation of men. In cultural revolution, however, this negation occurs simultaneously with the birth of the new culture in the womb of the old.

Both cultural action and cultural revolution imply communion between the leaders and the people, as subjects who are transforming reality. In cultural revolution, however, communion is so firm that the leaders and the people become like one body, checked by a permanent process of self-scrutiny.[28] Both cultural action and cultural revolution are founded on scientific knowledge of reality, but in cultural revolution, science is no longer at the service of domination. On two points, however, there is no distinction between cultural action for freedom and cultural revolution. Both are committed to 'conscientization', and the necessity for each is explained by the 'dialectic of overdetermination'.

We have spoken of the challenge facing Latin America in this period of historical transition. We believe that other areas of the Third World are no exception to what we have described, though each will present its own particular nuances. If the paths they follow are to lead to liberation, they cannot bypass cultural action for 'conscientization'. Only through such a process can the 'maximum of potential consciousness' be attained by the emergent and uncritical masses, and the passage from submersion in semi-intransitiveness to full emergence be achieved. If we have faith in men, we cannot be content with saying that they are human persons while doing nothing concrete to enable them to exist as such.

28. Even though these statements on cultural revolution can be applied to an analysis of the Chinese cultural revolution and beyond, that is not our intention. We restrict our study to a sketch of the relationship between cultural revolution and cultural action which we propose.

Appendix

We shall describe in this appendix how a generative word from a syllabic language is de-composed, and how new words are formed from it.

Generative word. A tri-syllabic word chosen from the 'linguistic universe' during research preliminary to the literacy course. Example: FAVELA ('slum').

Codification. The imaging of a significant aspect of a man's existential situation in a slum. The generative word is inserted in this codification. The codification functions as the knowable object mediating between the knowing subjects – the educator and learners – in the act of knowing they achieve in dialogue.

Real or concrete context. The slum reality as a framework for the objective facts which directly concern slum dwellers.

Theoretical context. The discussion group (*circulo de cultura*), in which the educators and learners – by means of the codification of the objective slum reality – engage in dialogue about the *reason* of the slum reality. The deeper this act of knowing goes, the more reality the learners unveil for what it is, discarding the myths which envelop it. This cognitive operation enables the learners to transform their interpretation of reality from mere opinion to a more critical knowledge.

Thus, as the theoretical context, the discussion group is the specialized environment where we submit the facts found in the concrete context, the slum, to critical analysis. The codification, representing those facts, is the knowable object. Decodification, breaking down the codified totality and putting it together again (retotalizing it), is the process by which the knowing subjects seek to know. The dialogical relationship is indispensable to this act.

Stages of de-codification

1. The knowing subjects begin the operation of breaking down the codified whole. This enables them to penetrate the whole in terms of the relationships among its parts, which until then the viewers did not perceive.

2. After a thorough analysis of the existential situation of the slum, the semantic relation between the generative word and what it signifies it established.

3. After the word has been seen in the situation, another slide is projected in which only the word appears, without the image of the situation: FAVELA.

4. The generative word is immediately separated into its syllables: FA VE LA

5. The 'family' of the first syllable is shown:
FA, FE, FI, FO, FU
Confronted with this syllabic family, the students identify only the syllable FA, which they know from the generative word. What is the next step for an educator who believes that learning to read and write is an act of knowing (who also knows that this is not, as for Plato, an act of remembering what has been forgotten)? He realizes that he must supply the students with new information, but he also knows that he must present the material to them as a problem. Thus, he poses two questions:

(a) Do these 'pieces' (the Brazilian students called the syllables 'pieces', and there was no reason why they should be made to call them syllables) have something that makes them alike and something that makes them different?
After a few moments in which the group looks at the slide in

silence, one will say, 'They all begin the same way, but they end differently.'

(b) At this moment, the educator asks another question: If they all begin the same way but end differently, can we call them all FA?

Again a brief silence; then, 'No!'

Only at this point, having prepared the learners critically for the information, does the educator supply it. Since it was preceded by a problem the information is not a mere gift.

6. Then comes the 'family' of the word's second syllable:
VA, VE, VI, VO, VU
The educator repeats the process. Some learners immediately say VA, VE, VI, VO, VU.

7. The 'family' of the third syllable:
LA, LE, LI, LO, LU
This slide is called the 'slide of discovery', a phrase coined by Professor Aurenice Cardoso, our assistant when we directed the National Plan for Adult Literacy in Brazil.

The educator proposes a horizontal and a vertical reading of the slide. This strengthens the learners' grasp of the vowel sounds *a, e, i, o, u*.

Next, the educator asks the learners: Do you think we can (never, do you think *you* can) create something with these pieces?

This is the decisive moment for learning. It is the moment when those learning to read and write discover the syllabic composition of words in their language.

After a silence, sometimes disconcerting to the inexperienced educator, the learners begin, one by one, to discover the words of their language by putting together the syllables in a variety of combinations: FAVELA, says one, FAVO, another; FIVELA; LUVA; LI; VALE; VALA; VIVA; FALO; FALE; FE; FAVA; VILA; LAVA; VELE; VELA; VIVE; VIVO; FALAVA; etc.

With the second generative word, the learners combine its syllables not only among themselves, but with those of the first word. Hence, knowing five or six generative words, the learners can begin to write brief notes. At the same time, however, they continue to discuss and critically analyse the real context as represented in the codifications.

This is what the primers cannot do. The authors of primers, as we have pointed out, choose generative words according to their own liking; they themselves decompose them; they themselves recombine their syllables to form new words, and with these words, they themselves evolve the phrases which generally echo the ones we have already quoted: *Eva viu a uva* ('Eva saw the grape'); *A asa é da ave* ('the bird's wing').

References

AFRICA TODAY, 'The role of poetry in the Mozambican revolution', vol. 16, no. 2, April–May, 1969.

SYLVIA ASHTON-WARNER (1966), *Teacher*, Penguin.

LOUIS ALTHUSSER (1970), *For Marx*, trans. B. Brewster, Allen Lane, The Penguin Press.

LOUIS ALTHUSSER and ETIENE BALIBAR (1969), *Para Leer el Capital*, Siglio XXI, Mexico.

JOHN BELOFF (1964), *The Existence of Mind*, MacGibbon & Kee.

HENRI BERGSON (1954), *The Two Sources of Morality and Religion*, trans R. A. Audra and C. Brereton, Doubleday.

FERNANDO HENRIQUE CARDOSO (1968), 'Hegemonia burguesa e independencia ecocomica raizes estruturias da crise politica brasileira', *Revista Civilzacão Brasileira*, no. 17, January.

PIERRE TEILHARD DE CHARDIN (1965), *The Appearance of Man*, trans. J. M. Cohen, Collins.

NOAM CHOMSKY (1966), *Cartesian Linguistics*, Harper & Row.

FRANTZ FANON (1968), *The Wretched of the Earth*, Penguin.

PAULO FREIRE (1970), 'Cultural freedom in Latin America', in *Human Rights and the Liberation of Man in the Americas*, edited by Louis M. Colonese, University of Notre Dame Press, Indiana.

PAULO FREIRE (1969), 'La alfabetizacion de adultos, critica de su vision ingenua, compreension de su vision crítica', *Introducion a la Accion Cultural*, ICIRA Santiago, Chile.

PAULO FREIRE (1972), *Pedagogy of the Oppressed*, Sheed & Ward; Penguin.

PAULO FREIRE (1969), *Annual Report: Activities for 1968*, ICIRA, Santiago, Chile. Trans. John Davitt, Center for Study of Development and Social Change, Cambridge, Massachusetts (mimeo).

PAULO FREIRE (1917), *Educação como Prática da Liberdade*, Paz e Terra, Rio de Janeiro.

ERICH FROMM (1965), *The Heart of Man*, Routledge & Kegan Paul.

LUCIEN GOLDMANN (1969), *The Human Science and Philosophy*, Cape.

ANTONIO GRAMSCI (1967), *Cultura y Literatura*, Ediciones Peninsula, Madrid.

LESZEK KOLAKOWSKI (1969), *Towards a Marxist Humanism*, Grove Press.

KAREL KOSIK (1967), *Dialectica de lo Concreto*, Grÿalbo, Mexico.

JOHN MACDERMOTT (1969), 'Technology: the opiate of intellectuals', *New York Review of Books*, vol. 13, no. 2, July.

GABRIEL MARCEL (1962), *Man Against Mass Society*, trans. G. S. Fraser, Regnery Gate.

KARL MARX (1946), *Capital*, ed. Frederick Engels, Allen & Unwin.

KARL MARX (1964), *Karl Marx, Selected Writings in Sociology and Social Philosophy*, trans. T. B. Bottomore, McGraw-Hill.

ALBERT MEMMI (1965), *Colonizer and the Colonized*, Orion Press.

KARL POPPER (1962), *The Open Society and Its Enemies*, Routledge & Kegan Paul.

ALBERTO GUERREIRO RAMON (1965), *A Redução Sociologica*. Instituto Superior de Estudios Brasileiros, Rio de Janeiro.

DARIO SALAS (1968), 'Algumas experiencias vividadas na Supervisao de Educacao basica', in *A Alfabetizao Functional oro Chile*, introduction by Paulo Freire, report to UNESCO, November.

JEAN-PAUL SARTRE (1947), *Situations 1*, Librairie Gallimard, Paris.

JEAN-PAUL SARTRE (1968), *Search for a Method*, trans. Hazel E. Barnes, Vintage Books.

UNESCO (1960) *La Situación Educativa en América Latina*, cuardo no. 20, Paris.

Pedagogy of the Oppressed
Paulo Freire

In Paulo Freire's hands literacy is a weapon for social change.
Education once again becomes the means by which men can
perceive, interpret, criticize and finally transform the world
about them.

Freire's attack on the 'culture of silence' inhabited by the vast
numbers of illiterate peasants in Brazil's poorest areas has
contributed in an extraordinary way to the development of a sense
of purpose and identity among the oppressed and demoralized
majority. His work is the result of a process of reflection in the
midst of a struggle to create a new social order. His is the
authentic voice of the Third World, but his methodology and
philosophy are also important in the industrialized countries where
a new culture of silence threatens to dominate an overconsuming
and overmanaged population, where education too often means
merely socialization. In contrast, Freire's approach concentrates
upon the ability to deal creatively with reality.

School Is Dead
Everett Reimer

Most of the children in the world are not in school. Most of
those who are drop out as soon as possible. Most countries
in the world can only afford to give their children the barest
minimum of education, while the costs of schooling are
everywhere rising faster than enrolments, and faster than national
income. Schools are for most people what the author calls
'institutional props for privilege', and yet at the same time they
are the major instruments of social mobility. But at what cost in
terms of true learning, true creativity, true democracy? And at
what ultimate cost to the societies which perpetuate themselves in
this way?

This is the background to Everett Reimer's important,
wide-ranging and intelligent book. The most urgent priority, he
argues, is for a consideration of *alternatives* in education –
alternative content, organization and finance. Above all, we
urgently need alternative views of education itself, its nature and
possible functions in the society of the future.

'Illich and Reimer have asked some of the profoundest
questions about education today'
Ian Lister-*The Times Higher Education Supplement*

'The case against universal compulsory schooling is a
substantial one and Everett Reimer thumps it out in chapter after
chapter'
Christopher Price, *New Statesman*

36 Children
Herbert Kohl

Herbert Kohl's 36 children were black twelve year olds in
New York's Harlem. From their standpoint school was an
irrelevance, to be treated sometimes with humour,
sometimes with lethargy, sometimes with dull, impotent,
insolent anger. From the standpoint of the educational
establishment they were 'the unteachable'. Herbert Kohl
was their teacher.

His achievement was to gain the confidence of his children
and to demonstrate that the world was more open to them
than their ghetto surroundings might suggest. Their innate
exuberance and liveliness come through in the series of
writings and drawings which form a major part of this book.
As Herbert Kohl makes clear, the process of educating
necessitated profound changes in his own sense of himself
as a teacher and a person. Few books on education give
such an inward view of what it is like to face an impossible
teaching situation and, in some measure, to come through.

'Desperate, angry, heartrending.... What Mr Kohl
discovered during that year ... is relevant to teaching
anywhere: marvellously exciting'
Edward Blishen, *New Statesman*

Pelican Latin American Library